40.95

CRITICAL PERSPECTIVES ON
CLIMATE CHANGE

ANALYZING THE ISSUES

CRITICAL PERSPECTIVES ON CLIMATE CHANGE

Edited by Stephen Feinstein

Enslow Publishing
101 W. 23rd Street
Suite 240
New York, NY 10011
USA

enslow.com

Published in 2017 by Enslow Publishing, LLC
101 W. 23rd Street, Suite 240, New York, NY 10011

Library of Congress Cataloging-in-Publication Data

Names: Feinstein, Stephen, editor.
Title: Critical perspectives on climate change / edited by Stephen Feinstein.
Description: New York, NY : Enslow Publishing, 2017. | "2017 | Series:
 Analyzing the issues | Includes bibliographical references and index.
Identifiers: LCCN 2016001573 | ISBN 9780766076709 (library bound)
Subjects: LCSH: Climatic changes—Juvenile literature. | Climatic
 changes—Effect of human beings on—Juvenile literature. | Climatic
 changes—Government policy—Juvenile literature. | Global warming—
 Juvenile literature.
Classification: LCC QC903.15 .C75 2017 | DDC 363.738/74—dc23
LC record available at http://lccn.loc.gov/2016001573

Printed in the United States of America

To Our Readers: We have done our best to make sure all website addresses in this book were active and appropriate when we went to press. However, the author and the publisher have no control over and assume no liability for the material available on those websites or on any websites they may link to. Any comments or suggestions can be sent by e-mail to customerservice@enslow.com.

Excerpts and articles have been reproduced with the permission of the copyright holders.

Photo Credits: Cover, YURI GRIPAS/AFP/Getty Images (climate change rally), Thaiview/Shutterstock.com (background, pp. 6–7 background), gbreezy/Shutterstock.com (magnifying glass on spine); p. 6 Ghornstern/Shutterstock.com (header design element, chapter start background throughout book).

CONTENTS

INTRODUCTION

Do you believe that global warming is occurring? If you do, you are in good company. According to a recent Yale/Gallup poll, at least 71 percent of Americans believe in the reality of global warming. About 57 percent of these people believe that this warming is the result of human activity. They understand this comes about mainly from the burning of fossil fuels, meaning oil, natural gas, and coal. The rest believe that global warming is at least partly caused by humans. Then there are those who agree global warming is occurring, caused by some natural process, but that there is nothing that can be done about it. And, of course, there are those who simply deny that climate change is even occurring at all.

Climate change in the form of global warming is recognized by a majority of the world's people as the greatest challenge facing humanity in the twenty-first century. Yet despite all the evidence of climate change, some people continue to doubt that global warming exists. Some skeptics are sincere in their belief. Others deny the existence of global warming because of vested interests in companies that contribute to global warming. Some have the mistaken impression that most scientists are global warming skeptics. Then there are those who acknowledge that the earth is warming, but believe that this is actually a good thing and will be quite beneficial! For example, some people state that the loss of sea ice in the Arctic Ocean will allow shipping along a polar route, and that a warmer climate in places such as Canada and Russia will result in increases in agricultural production due to a longer growing season. (Of course, the opposite situation would occur in lower latitudes, such as the United States, where decreasing rainfall will result in prolonged droughts and devastation to the nation's farmlands.)

There are reasons why many people are confused about climate change. The details of the natural atmospheric and oceanic processes involved in determining the climate are incredibly complex. Scientists using the most powerful supercomputers are still left with a great deal of uncertainty. Also, people sometimes confuse climate with weather.

Weather is what happens at a particular location on a particular day. The climate is the average of that weather over a long period of time. So if the climate for that place indicates cold snowy winters, you might be surprised by a winter day or week during which the temperatures rise into the 60s or 70s. And if you are used to hot, humid summers, unseasonably cool weather during July or August might lead you to believe that the earth is cooling rather than warming.

Also adding to the confusion of whether or not the Earth's climate is warming are the different conditions that occur in different parts of the planet. For example, in recent years, the Arctic is heating up faster than any other part of the planet. Huge areas of the Arctic Ocean have been losing immense amounts of ice. In late December of 2015, Russia's Ministry of Natural Resources and Environmental Protection revealed that the country is warming at 2.5 times the global average and faces a dramatic rise in related threats from floods and fires. Yet the northeast United States has recently experienced several unusually cold and snowy winters. After braving bitter cold winds while trudging through deep snow drifts clogging the streets, you might very well be inclined to dismiss global warming as total nonsense. So what can we make of this?

To help you form an opinion about climate change, let's look at how global warming might be occurring. According to most scientists, there is more than enough evidence for the existence of this phenomenon. And their conclusion is that the overall warming of the earth has picked up speed due to human activity. Here's how it works: Gases that exist naturally in Earth's atmosphere in the form of water vapor, carbon dioxide (CO_2), methane, and other trace gases absorb radiation from the sun. These gases trap heat in the atmosphere. People have compared this process to the way in which glass in a greenhouse traps heat. This is where the term "greenhouse gases" comes from.

Greenhouse gases are beneficial and, in fact, necessary. Indeed, greenhouse gases make the earth habitable for all forms of life, which means that we could not exist without it. But with the recent increase in these gases, we now have too much of a good thing. By burning fossil fuels, such as oil, gas, and coal, we have increased the greenhouse gases in the upper atmosphere, thus disrupting Earth's energy balance (e.g., radiation coming in versus radiation going out). Burning fossil fuels adds carbon dioxide to the atmosphere, which, in turn, strengthens the greenhouse effect. Other greenhouse gases, including methane and nitrous oxide, have been building up in the atmosphere and are also contributing to global warming. Agricultural activities and the burning of fossil fuels are responsible for the increased methane. Agriculture and the chemical industry are sources of nitrous oxide.

Greenhouse gases have already had a significant effect on Earth's climate. During the past one hundred years, the average global temperature has increased by about 0.5 degrees Celsius (1 degree Fahrenheit). One degree might not sound like much, but this change in temperature has already resulted in extremely serious climate change, including partial melting of the polar ice caps and many of the world's glaciers. But much worse is in store for us in the future. Even if somehow we could immediately halt all emissions of greenhouse gases (which of course is impossible), there is already enough of these gases in the atmosphere that warming will continue no matter what we do to reduce such emissions. Scientists say that by the end of this century, global temperatures could rise by an additional 4 degrees Celsius (7.2 degrees Fahrenheit), bringing about catastrophic climate change.

As awareness and concern about the ramifications of a warming planet grew among the world's nations, an international response was born. Influential political leaders and scientists realized that they had to find a way to set limits and reduce the amount of greenhouse gas emissions. And this was a project that required the cooperation and participation of all nations. Obviously, if only one or a few nations cut their burning of fossil fuels, this would do nothing to slow down or halt global warming.

In 1979, the first World Climate Conference took place. In 1992 at the Earth Summit in Rio de Janeiro, countries of the world joined an international treaty, the United Nations Framework Convention on Climate Change (UNFCCC), to consider what they could do to limit global temperature increases and the resulting climate change, and to cope with its impacts. By 1995, countries participating in the first Conference of the Parties (COP1) in Berlin realized that emission reductions provisions in the 1992 Convention were inadequate. As a result, they launched negotiations to strengthen the global response to climate change, and, in 1997, adopted the Kyoto Protocol at COP3. In the following years, world conferences on climate change were held in Marrakesh, Nairobi, and Bali. At COP15 in Copenhagen in 2009, countries agreed to non-binding emissions reductions pledges. Meetings continued over the next few years at Cancun, Durban, Doha, Warsaw, and Lima.

In December 2015, COP21 in Paris reached an agreement that, for many, finally held out some hope for progress against global warning. The milestone accord, signed by 195 countries, was the first time all countries agreed to join the fight against global warming. As we'll see, however, not all experts and climate activists believe that this was the most effective, or egalitarian, plan of action.

For all participants in the climate conferences, the issues and problems involved in trying to reach agreements have been extremely complex and difficult to resolve. It has become clear to many that the changing climate impacts just about every aspect of life on our planet, making already difficult problems worse. Environmental, economic, and political issues are all impacted, ultimately including questions of war or peace, and life or death.

So when it comes to climate change and what it could mean for you and me and the rest of humanity, there is obviously a lot to think about. This book includes thoughts on climate change from leading scientists, politicians, environmentalists, climate activists, businessmen, and spiritual leaders. Hopefully what these people have to say on the subject will help clarify the issues involved and guide you to your own conclusions.

CHAPTER 1

WHAT THE GOVERNMENT AND POLITICIANS SAY

Many of our political leaders, including President Obama, understand that global warming is real and that the government must implement a plan to deal with it.

Yet some who hold political office refuse to accept the scientific evidence for global warming. In January 2015, the National Aeronautics and Space Administration (NASA) and the National Oceanic and Atmospheric Administration (NOAA) declared 2014 the hottest year ever recorded on Earth. Several days later, rejecting the scientific consensus that humans are causing climate change, the Republican-controlled United States Senate went on record in a 50-49 vote saying that climate change is not caused by humans. Although according to NASA, 97 percent of scientists now believe that climate change is man-made, many Republican politicians disagree.

This chapter includes the thoughts of political leaders who weigh in on different sides of this debate, as well as news articles that analyze political rhetoric in order to get down to the facts of the issue.

"REMARKS BY PRESIDENT OBAMA AT THE GLACIER CONFERENCE — ANCHORAGE, AK," FROM WHITEHOUSE.GOV, SEPTEMBER 1, 2015

Dena'ina Civic and Convention Center Anchorage, Alaska

THE PRESIDENT: Thank you so much. Thank you. It is wonderful to be here in the great state of Alaska.

I want to thank Secretary Kerry and members of my administration for your work here today. Thank you to the many Alaskans, Alaska Natives and other indigenous peoples of the Arctic who've traveled a long way, in many cases, to share your insights and your experiences. And to all the foreign ministers and delegations who've come here from around the world — welcome to the United States, and thank you all for attending this GLACIER Conference.

The actual name of the conference is much longer. It's a mouthful, but the acronym works because it underscores the incredible changes that are taking place here in the Arctic that impact not just the nations that surround the Arctic, but have an impact for the entire world, as well.

I want to thank the people of Alaska for hosting this conference. I look forward to visiting more of Alaska over the next couple of days. The United States is, of course, an Arctic nation. And even if this isn't an official gathering of the Arctic Council, the United States is proud to chair the Arctic Council for the next two years. And to all the foreign dignitaries who are here, I want to be very clear — we are eager to work with your nations on the unique opportunities that the Arctic presents and the unique challenges that it faces. We are not going to — any of us — be able to solve these challenges by ourselves. We can only solve them together.

Of course, we're here today to discuss a challenge that will define the contours of this century more dramatically than any other — and that's the urgent and growing threat of a changing climate.

Our understanding of climate change advances each day. Human activity is disrupting the climate, in many ways faster than we previously thought. The science is stark. It is sharpening. It proves that this once-distant threat is now very much in the present.

In fact, the Arctic is the leading edge of climate change - our leading indicator of what the entire planet faces. Arctic temperatures are rising about twice as fast as the global average. Over the past 60 years, Alaska has warmed about twice as fast as the rest of the United States. Last year was Alaska's warmest year on record — just as it was for the rest of the world. And the impacts here are very real.

Thawing permafrost destabilizes the earth on which 100,000 Alaskans live, threatening homes, damaging transportation and energy infrastructure, which could cost billions of dollars to fix.

Warmer, more acidic oceans and rivers, and the migration of entire species, threatens the livelihoods of indigenous peoples, and local economies dependent on fishing and tourism. Reduced sea levels leaves villages unprotected from floods and storm surges. Some are in imminent danger; some will have to relocate entirely. In fact, Alaska has some of the swiftest shoreline erosion rates in the world.

I recall what one Alaska Native told me at the White House a few years ago. He said, "Many of our villages are ready to slide off into the waters of Alaska, and in some cases, there will be absolutely no hope -— we will need to move many villages."

Alaska's fire season is now more than a month longer than it was in 1950. At one point this summer, more than 300 wildfires were burning at once. Southeast of here, in our Pacific Northwest, even the rain forest is on fire. More than 5 million acres in Alaska have already been scorched by fire this year — that's an area about the size of Massachusetts. If you add the fires across Canada and Siberia, we're talking 300 [30] million acres -— an area about the size of New York.

This is a threat to many communities — but it's also an immediate and ongoing threat to the men and women who put their lives on the line to protect ours. Less than two weeks ago, three highly trained firefighters lost their lives fighting a fire in Washington State. Another has been in critical condition. We are thankful to each and every firefighter for their heroism — including the Canadian firefighters who've helped fight the fires in this state.

But the point is that climate change is no longer some far-off problem. It is happening here. It is happening now. Climate change is already disrupting our agriculture and ecosystems, our water and food supplies, our energy, our infrastructure, human health, human safety — now. Today. And climate change is a trend that affects all trends — economic trends, security trends. Everything will be impacted. And it becomes more dramatic with each passing year.

Already it's changing the way Alaskans live. And considering the Arctic's unique role in influencing the global climate, it will accelerate changes to the way that we all live.

Since 1979, the summer sea ice in the Arctic has decreased by more than 40 percent — a decrease that has dramatically accelerated over the past two decades. One new study estimates that Alaska's glaciers alone lose about 75 gigatons — that's 75 billion tons — of ice each year.

To put that in perspective, one scientist described a gigaton of ice as a block the size of the National Mall in Washington — from Congress all the way to the Lincoln Memorial, four times as tall as the Washington Monument. Now imagine 75 of those ice blocks. That's what Alaska's glaciers alone lose each year. The pace of melting is only getting faster. It's now twice what it was between 1950 and 2000 — twice as fast as it was just a little over a decade ago. And it's one of the reasons why sea levels rose by about eight inches over the last century, and why they're projected to rise another one to four feet this century.

Consider, as well, that many of the fires burning today are actually burning through the permafrost in the Arctic. So this permafrost stores massive amounts of carbon. When the permafrost is no longer permanent, when it thaws or burns, these gases are released into our atmosphere over time, and that could mean that the Arctic may become a new source of emissions that further accelerates global warming.

So if we do nothing, temperatures in Alaska are projected to rise between six and 12 degrees by the end of the century, triggering more melting, more fires, more thawing of the permafrost, a negative feedback loop, a cycle — warming leading to more warming — that we do not want to be a part of.

And the fact is that climate is changing faster than our efforts to address it. That, ladies and gentlemen, must change. We're not acting fast enough.

I've come here today, as the leader of the world's largest economy and its second largest emitter, to say that the United States recognizes our role in creating this problem, and we embrace our responsibility to help solve it. And I believe we can solve it. That's the good news. Even if we cannot reverse the damage that we've already caused, we have the means — the scientific imagination and technological innovation — to avoid irreparable harm.

We know this because last year, for the first time in our history, the global economy grew and global carbon emissions stayed flat. So we're making progress; we're just not making it fast enough.

Here in the United States, we're trying to do our part. Since I took office six and a half years ago, the United States has made ambitious investments in clean energy, and ambitious reductions in our carbon emissions. We now harness three times as much electricity from wind and 20 times as much from the sun. Alaskans now lead the world in the development of hybrid wind energy systems from remote grids, and it's expanding its solar and biomass resources.

We've invested in energy efficiency in every imaginable way — in our buildings, our cars, our trucks, our homes, even the appliances inside them. We're saving consumers billions of dollars along the way. Here in Alaska, more than 15,000 homeowners have cut their energy bills by 30 percent on average. That collectively saves Alaskans more than $50 million each year. We've helped communities build climate-resilient infrastructure to prepare for the impacts of climate change that we can no longer prevent.

Earlier this month, I announced the first set of nationwide standards to end the limitless dumping of carbon pollution from our power plants. It's the single most important step America has ever taken on climate change. And over the course of the coming days, I intend to speak more about the particular challenges facing Alaska and the United States as an Arctic power, and I intend to announce new measures to address them.

So we are working hard to do our part to meet this challenge. And in doing so, we're proving that there doesn't have to be a conflict between a sound environment and strong economic growth. But we're not moving fast enough. None of the nations represented here are moving fast enough.

And let's be honest — there's always been an argument against taking action. The notion is somehow this will curb our economic growth. And at a time when people are anxious about the economy, that's an argument often-times for inaction. We don't want our lifestyles disrupted. In countries where there remains significant poverty, including here in the United States, the notion is, can we really afford to prioritize this issue. The irony, of course, is, is that few things will disrupt our lives as profoundly as climate change. Few things can have as negative an impact on our economy as climate change.

On the other hand, technology has now advanced to the point where any economic disruption from transitioning to a cleaner, more efficient economy is shrinking by the day. Clean energy and energy efficiency aren't just proving cost-effective, but also cost-saving. The unit costs of things like solar are coming down rapidly. But we're still underinvesting in it.

Many of America's biggest businesses recognize the opportunities and are seizing them. They're choosing a new route. And a growing number of American home-owners are choosing to go solar every day. It works. All told, America's economy has grown more than 60 percent over the last 20 years, but our carbon emissions are roughly back to where they were 20 years ago. So we know how to use less dirty fuel and grow our economy at the same time. But we're not moving fast enough.

More Americans every day are doing their part, though. Thanks to their efforts, America will reach the emission target that I set six years ago. We're going to reduce our carbon emissions in the range of 17 percent below 2005 levels by 2020. And that's why, last year, I set a new target: America is going to reduce our emissions 26 to 28 percent below 2005 levels by 10 years from now.

And that was part of a historic joint announcement we made last year in Beijing. The United States will double the pace at which we cut our emissions, and China committed, for the first time, to limiting its emissions. Because the world's two largest economies and two largest emitters came together, we're now seeing other nations stepping up aggressively as well. And I'm determined to make sure American leadership continues to drive international action — because we can't do this alone. Even America and China together cannot do this alone. Even all the countries represented around here cannot do this alone. We have to do it together.

This year, in Paris, has to be the year that the world finally reaches an agreement to protect the one planet that we've got while we still can.

So let me sum up. We know that human activity is changing the climate. That is beyond dispute. Everything else is politics if people are denying the facts of climate change. We can have a legitimate debate about how we are going to address this problem; we cannot deny the science. We also know the devastating consequences if the current trend lines continue. That is not deniable. And we are going to have to do some adaptation, and we are going to have to help communities be resilient, because of these trend lines we are not going to be able to stop on a dime. We're not going to be able to stop tomorrow.

But if those trend lines continue the way they are, there's not going to be a nation on this Earth that's not impacted negatively. People will suffer. Economies will suffer. Entire nations will find themselves under severe, severe problems. More drought; more floods; rising sea levels; greater migration; more refugees; more scarcity; more conflict.

That's one path we can take. The other path is to embrace the human ingenuity that can do something about it. This is within our power. This is a solvable problem if we start now.

And we're starting to see that enough consensus is being built internationally and within each of our body politics that we may have the political will – finally – to get moving.

So the time to heed the critics and the cynics and the deniers is past. The time to plead ignorance is surely past. Those who want to ignore the science, they are increasingly alone. They're on their own shrinking island.

And let's remember, even beyond the climate benefits of pursuing cleaner energy sources and more resilient, energy-efficient ways of living, the byproduct of it is, is that we also make our air cleaner and safer for our children to breathe. We're also making our economies more resilient to energy shocks on global markets. We're also making our countries less reliant on unstable parts of the world. We are gradually powering a planet on its way to 9 billion humans in a more sustainable way. These are good things. This is not simply a danger to be avoided; this is an opportunity to be seized. But we have to keep going. We're making a difference, but we have to keep going. We are not moving fast enough.

If we were to abandon our course of action, if we stop trying to build a clean-energy economy and reduce carbon pollution, if we do nothing to keep the glaciers from melting faster, and oceans from rising faster, and forests from burning faster, and storms from growing stronger, we will condemn our children to a planet beyond their capacity to repair: Submerged countries. Abandoned cities. Fields no longer growing. Indigenous peoples who can't carry out traditions that stretch back millennia. Entire industries of people who can't practice their livelihoods. Desperate refugees seeking the sanctuary of nations not their own. Political disruptions that could trigger multiple conflicts around the globe.

That's not a future of strong economic growth. That is not a future where freedom and human rights are on the move. Any leader willing to take a gamble on a future like that—any so-called leader who does not take this issue seriously or treats it like a joke—is not fit to lead.

On this issue, of all issues, there is such a thing as being too late. That moment is almost upon us. That's why we're here today. That's what we have to convey to our people— tomorrow, and the next day, and the day after that. And that's what we have to do when we meet in Paris later this year. It will not be easy. There are hard questions to answer. I am not trying to suggest that there are not going to be difficult transitions that we all have to make. But if we unite our highest aspirations, if we make our best efforts to protect this planet for future genera-tions, we can solve this problem.

And when you leave this conference center, I hope you look around. I hope you have the chance to visit a glacier. Or just look out your airplane window as you depart, and take in the God-given majesty of this place. For those of you flying to other parts of the world, do it again when you're flying over your home countries. Remind yourself that there will come a time when your grandkids—and mine, if I'm lucky enough to have some— they'll want to see this. They'll want to experience it, just as we've gotten to do in our own lives. They deserve to live lives free from fear, and want, and peril. And ask your-self, are you doing everything you can to protect it. Are we doing everything we can to make their lives safer, and more secure, and more prosperous?

Let's prove that we care about them and their long-term futures, not just short-term political expediency.

I had a chance to meet with some Native peoples before I came in here, and they described for me villages that are slipping into the sea, and the changes that are taking place—changing migratory patterns; the changing fauna so that what used to feed the animals that they, in turn, would hunt or fish beginning to vanish. It's urgent for them today. But that is the future for all of us if we don't take care.

Your presence here today indicates your recogni-tion of that. But it's not enough just to have conferences. It's not enough just to talk the talk. We've got to walk the walk. We've got work to do, and we've got to do it together.

So, thank you. And may God bless all of you, and your countries. And thank you, Alaska, for your wonderful hospitality. Thank you.

1. Why did President Obama refer to the Arctic as the "leading edge of climate change"?

2. According to President Obama, what will be impacted by climate change?

"ETHICS ON FILM: DISCUSSION OF *AN INCONVENIENT TRUTH*," BY THE CARNEGIE COUNCIL FOR ETHICS IN INTERNATIONAL AFFAIRS, FROM WWW.CARNEGIECOUNCIL.ORG

OVERVIEW

In 2007 Al Gore shared the Nobel Peace Prize with the United Nations' Intergovernmental Panel on Climate Change (IPCC). The Nobel Committee cited Gore's long-standing commitment to raising public awareness of global warming and of the changes needed to prevent it from worsening. His most well-known work to date on these issues is this film.

Gore has been an environmental activist for decades. He became convinced of the reality of climate change during his college days in the 1960s and organized the first Congressional hearings on global warming in 1976. Since 1990 he has been giving a slideshow on global warming to audiences around the world, and much of *An Inconvenient Truth* is footage of the most recent incar-nation of his presentation. This sounds like a recipe for boredom, but in fact the movie is gripping. The graphics are sophisticated, the images terrifying, and Gore makes the mass of facts and statistics meaningful and dramatic. To lighten the grim mood, he cracks jokes and even uses cartoons from time to time to illustrate scientific concepts.

Gore also uses his human side to bring the points home. Deftly interweaving his own personal and political history, he describes the events in his life that led him to care so deeply about the issue and then links them to the bigger picture. For example, he relates how his family didn't stop growing tobacco until after his older sister's death in 1984 from lung cancer, and explains how this helped him understand the human tendency to resist changing one's habits until something goes terribly wrong. "It's human nature to take time to connect the dots," he says, "but eventually there's a day of reckoning."

After over an hour of apocalyptic images, the film ends on a rousing and hopeful note. "We already know everything we need to know to solve this problem," declares Gore. "We have everything we need except political will—and that's a renewable resource." Calling this the "moral issue of our time," Gore says that Americans have risen to the occasion before and they can do so again. In sum, the solutions he proposes are to emit less greenhouse gases by saving energy, and to absorb more gases by planting trees and vegetation. He ends by calling on the audience to learn more about ways to help.

IS THE FILM PARTISAN?

Gore stresses that the issue of global warming is not and should not be treated as a partisan one, yet he cannot resist making cutting remarks about the Bush administration from time to time, some joking, some very serious. For example, he discusses Philip Cooney, formerly chief of staff to President Bush's Council on Environmental Quality and, before that, a lobbyist for the American Petroleum Institute, who resigned in 2005 after it was revealed that he had edited government reports on climate change, downplaying the role of carbon dioxide emissions.

Nevertheless, although some may disagree with the science and/or resent Gore's comments about the Republicans, no one could mistake this film for a partisan polemic. Gore is passionate to convince everyone of whatever political stripe that we are witnessing a global catastrophe in the making. It can be averted, he argues, but only through collective action, on both the personal and political level.

THE U.S. AND THE KYOTO PROTOCOL

As Vice-President, Gore successfully advocated for the implementation of a carbon tax, but he failed to persuade the Senate to agree to ratify the Kyoto Protocol of the United Nations Framework Convention on Climate Change (UNFCC) in 1997. The sticking point, then as now, was that there were no binding targets and requirements for developing nations to reduce emissions, combined with fears about the effect on the U.S. economy. In 1998, Gore signed the Protocol as a symbolic gesture. At present the U.S. remains a signatory to the Kyoto Protocol but the signature alone remains symbolic, as the Protocol is non-binding on the U.S. unless ratified. As of November 2007, 174 countries and other government entities had ratified the Protocol. Among them are 137 developing countries, including China and India, but these developing nations have no obligation beyond monitoring and reporting emissions.

REACTIONS TO THE FILM

The reaction of climate scientists to the film has been mixed. The majority of them believe that the human contribution to global warming is significant and therefore many endorse the film, although with varying degrees of qualification. Some point to minor errors, such as Gore's claim that the effects of the U.S. Clean Air Act, as registered in aerosol concentrations in Antarctic ice cores, are visible to the naked eye (they are not), but they underscore that such errors take nothing away from the film's main conclusions.

Others have expressed concern over what they see as 'alarmist' elements of the film, such as its portrayal of future coastal flooding due to the melting of Greenland as something "impending." Scientists estimate that if carbon dioxide emissions continue at their current rate, it would take at least 500 to 1000 years for Greenland to completely melt.

Nevertheless, according to the Intergovernmental Panel on Climate Change (IPCC), by 2080 sea level could rise from 9 to 48 cm in a 'Low Emissions Scenario' and from 16 to 69 cm in a 'High Emissions Scenario.' The IPCC confirms that sea level rise is already affecting coastal ecosystems, including coral reefs, mangroves and salt-marshes. Two uninhabited Pacific islands have already disappeared and others are becoming uninhabitable (see Sea Level Rise by the World Wildlife Fund.)

A relatively small group of climate scientists disputes that human activities contribute in any significant way to global warming. This group, naturally, rejects the main conclusions of the film.

For more on scientists' views of the film and negative reactions from global warming skeptics (some funded by oil companies), read "Did Al Get the Science Right?, June 2006.

In addition to the Oscar, the film won a number of other awards. As of June 3, 2007, it had grossed over $24 million in the U.S. and over $49 million worldwide, making it the fourth-highest-grossing documentary in the U.S. to date.

Not all politicians around the world were positive about the film, however, and in some areas there has been controversy about showing it in schools.

ETHICAL ISSUES AND DISCUSSION QUESTIONS

1. Do you find this film convincing, and if so, will you take action in any way to help reduce emissions? If you don't agree with the film's conclusions, what are your reasons?

2. Gore declares that there is a moral imperative to act to reduce the greenhouse gas emissions that cause global warming. He suggests that the moral imperative derives from a duty we have to leave to future generations a planet as habitable as the one we inherited from our ancestors. What is the exact nature of this duty?

3. A principal reason that the U.S. government gave for not ratifying the Kyoto Protocol was that it would harm the U.S. economy. For example, legislative measures requiring power plants to substantially increase their use of renewable energy sources could result in many workers losing their jobs, as well as increasing consumer prices. Gore insists that the economy versus the planet is a false choice. Do you agree? Amidst fears of job loss and recession and without absolute consensus in the scientific community as to the role of

carbon dioxide emissions in global warming, let alone popular consensus, how can such legislative measures be justified?

4. Another reason that the U.S. has not ratified the Kyoto Protocol is that it does not require other big polluters, such as China and India, to reduce their emissions. A chart in the film shows the U.S. as having the highest carbon emissions per capita in the world—more than five times the global average—and another shows the U.S. as being the greatest overall contributor to global warming. Today the U.S. still has the highest carbon emissions per capita in the world, but China is now the biggest emitter overall. According to a report by the Netherlands Environmental Agency, China's CO_2 emissions surpassed those of the USA by 8% in 2006.

5. However, part of the explanation for the rise of emissions in countries such as China, is that along with outsourcing jobs, the developed world is also outsourcing polluting industries to countries with lower pollution (and safety) standards. Given their high per capita emissions, does the U.S. and the rest of the developed world have an obligation to reduce emissions more rapidly than developing countries? What are some ways that it can help China, India, and the rest of the developing world to reduce their emissions?

6. One of the reasons for global warming, says Gore, is the continuing population explosion, which is projected to reach over 9 billion by 2050. What steps, if any, should the United States and other countries be taking to stabilize population growth?

7. Gore reports that in a survey of over 900 peer-reviewed articles on global warming published in respected sci-

entific journals, not one denied that global warming is occurring or that carbon dioxide emissions from the burning of fossil fuels is its most likely cause.

On the other hand, in a survey of articles on global warming in the U.S. popular press, over 50 percent questioned global warming or the role played by carbon dioxide emissions. In light of this, can the general public be faulted for not doing more to reverse the trend of global warming? Can policymakers? Have popular attitudes changed since the film was made? On this point, what do you make of the 2007 findings of WorldPublicOpinion.org?

8. What do you think would be the most effective ways to collectively reduce emissions?

1. Al Gore states that climate change is a non-partisan issue. Do you think this is correct?

2. Why might some political leaders prefer to ignore evidence of global warming?

"WHY MOST OF WHAT YOU THINK YOU KNOW ABOUT THE PARIS CLIMATE DEAL IS WRONG: AN ANNOTATED NEWS STORY," BY AVI LEWIS AND RAJIV SICORA, FROM *THE LEAP*, DECEMBER 19, 2015

With a little distance from the COP21 climate negotiations in Paris, it's clear that the meaning of the deal struck there is deeply contested. From the euphoric pronouncements of politicians like U.S. President Obama (this is "the best chance we have to save the one planet that we've got") to the scathing dismissal of climate scientist James Hansen (it's a "fraud"), lots of people reading the coverage of the agreement are understandably confused about what to make of it.

As independent journalists who were in Paris for the duration of the talks, following the twists and turns of the negotiations, we've been dismayed (if not surprised) by how faithfully large news organizations have reported spin as fact.

So in the spirit of correcting the record, we've annotated parts of a typical news story on the deal. While we chose the New York Times, we could easily have done the same for any of the major wire services or other big news organizations: the coverage was by and large as homogenous as it was inaccurate.

(Editor's note: The original article appears in italics here)

NATIONS APPROVE LANDMARK CLIMATE ACCORD IN PARIS

By CORAL DAVENPORT
DEC. 12, 2015
LE BOURGET, France — With the sudden bang of a gavel Saturday night, representatives of 195 nations reached a landmark accord that will, for the first time, commit nearly every country to lowering planet-warming greenhouse gas emissions to help stave off the most drastic effects of climate change.

If only this were true. In fact, the agreement does not commit countries to lowering emissions. To be sure, the text "invites," "recommends," "encourages," "requests," "further requests," and even "urges" countries to do a number of procedural things. And there are reporting requirements. But the key obligation on each one is to submit goals that it "intends to achieve." As long as a country's goals are regularly updated, and as long as governments "pursue" actions "with the aim of achieving the objectives," they are all free to completely fail to lower emissions without consequence.

The deal, which was met with an eruption of cheers and ovations from thousands of delegates gathered from around the world, represents a historic breakthrough on an issue that has foiled decades of international efforts to address climate change.

Given that the deal just binds countries to a process, rather than actual results, the smog of self-congratulation has been surprisingly thick. John Kerry boasted that it would "prevent the worst, most devastating consequences of climate change from ever happening." Al

Gore called it a "universal and ambitious agreement," and insisted that the era of "sustainable economic growth is now firmly and inevitably underway."

We learned from Richard Branson that "the course of history has shifted"—thanks to "the world's greatest diplomatic success," as a headline in The Guardian proclaimed. Bloggers like Jonathan Chait called it "one of the great triumphs in history." Economists like Jeffrey Sachs said that "agreements such as these appeal to our better angels" and called on us to "hail the Paris climate change agreement and get to work."

Traditionally, such pacts have required developed economies like the United States to take action to lower greenhouse gas emissions, but they have exempted developing countries like China and India from such obligations.

The accord, which United Nations diplomats have been working toward for nine years, changes that dynamic by requiring action in some form from every country, rich or poor.

Actually, the deal changes the dynamic by all but erasing the crucial principle of equity from the climate regime.

The Paris deal pays lip service to the idea of "common but differentiated responsibilities" (CBDR), which was a bedrock of the UN climate convention that began these talks in 1992. It says that the richest, long-time polluters are obligated to cut emissions first and deepest, while providing climate finance for poor countries, where people are the least culpable and the most vulnerable.

But inside the Paris talks, wealthy countries launched a determined assault on that idea, waging a successful campaign to shift far more of the burden onto the countries of the global South. That's not going to be a helpful "dynamic" in the years ahead, particularly because many of those developing countries are already leading on climate policy—another under-reported fact that is key to understanding the true nature of the Paris deal.

According to a landmark civil society review of current climate pledges, when you factor in each country's responsibility for historical emissions and its capacity to pay for climate action, developing countries—including China and India—are already doing their fair share (or even more). Rich countries are not. The US and EU have each pledged roughly a fifth of their fair shares.

"This is truly a historic moment," the United Nations secretary general, Ban Ki-moon, said in an interview. *"For the first time, we have a truly universal agreement on climate change, one of the most crucial problems on earth."*

WHAT DOES A CLIMATE DEAL MEAN FOR THE WORLD?

A group of 195 nations reached a landmark climate agreement on Saturday. Here is what it means for the planet, business, politics and other areas.

President Obama, who regards tackling climate change as a central element of his legacy, spoke of the deal in a televised address from the White House. "This agreement sends a powerful signal that the world is fully committed to a low-carbon future," he said. "We've shown that the world has both the will and the ability to take on this challenge."

As Obama crafts his climate legacy, the U.S. role in the negotiations has been woefully under-reported. One of the key U.S. goals in Paris was to rule out liability or mandatory compensation for climate damages in poor countries. To help push through that and other demands, Obama's negotiators cynically dangled support for a temperature target of 1.5 degrees Celsius—the goal that low-lying island and African nations have long fought for, given that their survival is at stake.

It seems that was enough to convince many poor countries to drop their demand for a strong "loss and damage" mechanism that could have been an immediate, concrete lifeline for countries hardest hit by the climate crisis. And in the end, of course, the "carrot" of 1.5 degrees was withdrawn and the very weakest language related to the temperature target was adopted. The final deal sets a goal of "well below" 2 degrees Celsius, adding only that governments should "pursue efforts" to meet the 1.5 target.

But the damage to "loss and damage" had been done.

The U.S. was also behind a last-minute "technical correction" announced at the scene of celebration at the final plenary. While this was presented in many news accounts as the great grammatical catch that saved a global climate deal, it actually marked the final watering down of the text. The U.S. insisted on changing the word "shall" (legally binding) to "should" (clearly not) in a crucial section: the duty of industrialized countries like the U.S. to take the lead on cutting emissions. From the beginning of the negotiations process in Paris, developing countries found themselves outmaneuvered and outnumbered, with smaller delegations struggling to keep up with the dozens of closed-door sessions happening at any one time. Civil society organizations and frontline voices, meanwhile, were often simply shut out.

Scientists and leaders said the talks here represented the world's last, best hope of striking a deal that would begin to avert the most devastating effects of a warming planet.

Mr. Ban said there was "no Plan B" if the deal fell apart. The Eiffel Tower was illuminated with that phrase Friday night.

The new deal will not, on its own, solve global warming. At best, scientists who have analyzed it say, it will cut global greenhouse gas emissions by about half enough as is necessary to stave off an increase in atmospheric temperatures of 2 degrees Celsius or 3.6 degrees Fahrenheit. That is the point at which, scientific studies have concluded, the world will be locked into a future of devastating consequences, including rising sea levels, severe droughts and flooding, widespread food and water shortages and more destructive storms.

In fact, one of the most remarkable features of the agreement is that it makes a point of highlighting its own inadequacy, noting that "much greater emission reduction efforts will be required" to meet even the 2 degree temperature target—and that current country commitments will likely lead to a 3 or even 4 degree temperature rise. That level of climate change, experts say, is "incompatible with any reasonable characterization of an organized, equitable and civilized global community."

No major news organization felt that this fact might serve as a strong lead. But even buried deep in a news story, it puts all the triumphalism in a different light. This is a special breed of "historic breakthrough," one that asserts itself as totally insufficient and that happens to put us on a path to apocalypse.

But the Paris deal could represent the moment at which, because of a shift in global economic policy, the inexorable rise in planet-warming carbon emissions that started during the Industrial Revolution began to level out and eventually decline.

At the same time, the deal could be viewed as a signal to global financial and energy markets, triggering a fundamental shift away from investment in coal, oil and gas as primary energy sources toward zero-carbon energy sources like wind, solar and nuclear power.

This is an interpretation shared by both politicians and many large environmental groups. It is clear that climate campaigners will be using the deal to pressure governments to make precisely this kind of historic shift.

But again, the text itself tells a different story. It never mentions fossil fuels. Not once. The phrase "renewable energy" appears a single time.

In fact, in the definition of the long-term emissions reduction goal (the absolute weakest option that had been on the table in Paris), we catch a glimpse of the future envisioned by the parties. The text says that countries will "aim" for a "balance between anthropogenic emissions by sources and removals by sinks of greenhouse gases in the second half of this century."

First of all, experts are pretty unequivocal that we should be entirely off of fossil fuels by mid-century. By introducing the notion that, post 2050, we can balance emissions with the removal of carbon from the atmosphere, the Paris deal keeps the door wide open for fossil fuel corporations to continue polluting, as long as they try to develop unproven and risky technologies to capture carbon and store it somewhere. This language also throws a lifeline to carbon trading schemes with so-called "offsets," which have failed miserably at reducing emissions, while too often displacing communities from their traditional lands to clear the way for monocrop plantations.

INSIDE THE PARIS CLIMATE DEAL

There's a lot we could say about the historical and political context of these talks, but we'll stick to the deal itself. Skip ahead a bit for the next comment.

Highlights from the final draft text of a climate agreement submitted to the delegates in Paris.

"The world finally has a framework for cooperating on climate change that's suited to the task," said Michael Levi, an expert on energy and climate change policy at the Council on Foreign Relations. "Whether or not this becomes a true turning point for the world, though, depends critically on how seriously countries follow through."

Just five years ago, such a deal seemed politically impossible. A similar 2009 climate change summit meeting in Copenhagen collapsed in acrimonious failure after countries could not unite around a deal.

Unlike in Copenhagen, Foreign Minister Laurent Fabius of France said on Saturday, the stars for this assembly were aligned.

The changes that led to the Paris accord came about through a mix of factors, particularly major shifts in the domestic politics and bilateral relationships of China and the United States, the world's two largest greenhouse gas polluters.

Since the Copenhagen deal collapsed, scientific studies have confirmed that the earliest impacts of climate change have started to sweep across the planet. While scientists once warned that climate change was a problem for future generations, recent scientific reports have concluded that it has started to wreak havoc now, from flooding in Miami to droughts and water shortages in China.

In a remarkable shift from their previous standoffs over the issue, senior officials from both the United States and China praised the Paris accord on Saturday night.

Representatives of the "high-ambition coalition," including Foreign Minister Tony de Brum of the Marshall Islands, left, wore lapel pins made of dried coconut fronds, a symbol of Mr. de Brum's country.

Secretary of State John Kerry, who has spent the past year negotiating behind the scenes with his Chinese and Indian counterparts in order to help broker the deal, said, "The world has come together around an agreement that will empower us to chart a new path for our planet."

Xie Zhenhua, the senior Chinese climate change negotiator, said, "The agreement is not perfect, and there are some areas in need of improvement." But he added, "This does not prevent us from marching forward with this historic step." Mr. Xie called the deal "fair and just, comprehensive and balanced, highly ambitious, enduring and effective."

Negotiators from many countries have said that a crucial moment in the path to the Paris accord came last year in the United States, when Mr. Obama enacted the nation's first climate change policy — a set of stringent new Environmental Protection Agency regulations designed to slash greenhouse gas pollution from the nation's coal-fired power plants. Meanwhile, in China, the growing internal criticism over air pollution from coal-fired power plants led President Xi Jinping to pursue domestic policies to cut coal use.

In November 2014 in Beijing, Mr. Obama and Mr. Xi announced that they would jointly pursue plans to cut domestic greenhouse gas emissions. That breakthrough announcement was seen as paving the way to the Paris deal, in which nearly all the world's nations have jointly announced similar plans.

The final language did not fully satisfy everyone. Representatives of some developing nations expressed consternation. Poorer countries had pushed for a legally binding provision requiring that rich countries appropriate a minimum of at least $100 billion a year to help them mitigate and adapt to the ravages of climate change. In the final deal, that $100 billion figure appears only in a preamble, not in the legally binding portion of the agreement.

The way it treats climate finance is another major failing of the Paris deal, though it has received little attention in the reporting. In fact, a little context makes this development even starker.

For developing countries, this issue has been one of the crucial sticking points in negotiations for the last decade. The Paris deal represents a huge step backwards.

First of all, the goal of $100 billion a year has been weakened, with developed countries striking any mention of "new" or "additional" funding from the legally-binding part of the agreement. There is no real process for strengthening existing finance commitments.

And even those existing commitments are not being honored. Not even close. Much of the $100 billion was supposed to be channeled through the "Green Climate Fund," created in 2010. It took 4 years for pledges to the fund to reach a mere $10 billion. By the start of the Paris talks, less than $1 billion had actually been collected, and a first round of projects amounting to a grand total of $168 million was hurriedly approved.

Finally, the goal of raising $100 billion per year was woefully inadequate to begin with. According to the International Energy Agency, in order to meet the 2 degree goal, annual green energy and efficiency investments need to be approaching $1 *trillion* by 2020, with most new spending happening in the developing world.

"We've always said that it was important that the $100 billion was anchored in the agreement," said Tosi Mpanu-Mpanu, a negotiator for the Democratic Republic of Congo and the incoming leader of a coalition known as the Least Developed Countries coalition. In the end, though, they let it go.

Despite the historic nature of the Paris climate accord, its success still depends heavily on two factors outside the parameter of the deal: global peer pressure and the actions of future governments.

The core of the Paris deal is a requirement that every nation take part. Ahead of the Paris talks, governments of 186 nations put forth public plans detailing how they would cut carbon emissions through 2025 or 2030.

Those plans alone, once enacted, will cut emissions by half the levels required to stave off the worst effects of global warming. The national plans vary vastly in scope and ambition—while every country is required to put forward a plan, there is no legal requirement dictating how, or how much, countries should cut emissions.

Thus, the Paris pact has built in a series of legally binding requirements that countries ratchet up the stringency of their climate change policies in the future. Countries will be required to reconvene every five years, starting in 2020, with updated plans that would tighten their emissions cuts.

Countries will also be legally required to reconvene every five years starting in 2023 to publicly report on how they are doing in cutting emissions compared to their plans. They will be legally required to monitor and report on their emissions levels and reductions, using a universal accounting system.

We can't afford to wait years for our global political class *to "ratchet up" its ambition. Thankfully, countless movements around the world are already leading the way, today, where the real action is—keeping fossil fuels in the ground and championing alternatives, whether it's kicking Shell out of the Arctic or building community wind and solar from Germany to Bangladesh. Every week, these movements are racking up new victories, building pressure from below for governments to take the kind of ambitious action that the crisis—and the science—demands.*

And that is where we see the best hope of urgent, immediate climate action: local victories building momentum and power, politicians taking their cue and implementing scaled-up policy frameworks that translate those breakthroughs to the regional and national levels.

A great example is the city of Portland, where years of local victories against coal export terminals and Arctic drilling schemes have culminated in the municipal government passing a resolution against any new fossil fuel infrastructure. And now cities across the Pacific Northwest of the U.S. are discussing doing the same.

There is nothing triumphant about declarations of intent at diplomatic confabs. But as movements ratchet up the pressure on the politicians who spoke such fine words in Paris, history could indeed be written in the wake of this deal.

And it better be. We need to see signs of genuine, real-world progress before the "Conference of the Parties serving as the meeting of the Parties to the Paris Agreement…take[s] stock of the implementation of this Agreement to assess the collective progress towards achieving the purpose of this Agreement and its long-term goals" in eight long, hot years' time.

1. Why do you think Avi Lewis and Rajiv Sicora went to all the trouble of annotating the article in the *New York Times?*

CHAPTER 2

WHAT SCIENTISTS SAY

Today, at least 97 percent of all scientists and 100 percent of climate scientists are convinced that global warming is real and that it presents a great danger. A relative handful of scientists who deny that humans are responsible for the changing climate point to other possible causes. Perhaps the sun has entered a period of greater energy output, allowing more solar radiation to reach the earth. After all, the climate has changed many times before in the earth's past. There were previous periods of much warmer temperatures long before the existence of humans, and there were also ice ages. Indeed, even throughout the history of the human race, there have been major fluctuations in the Earth's climate.

For example, a warm period lasting from 1000 CE to about 1350 CE is known as the Medieval Warm Period. From the years 1400 until about 1860, the earth's climate was so cold that the period is called the Little Ice Age. But none of these historical periods compare to what is occurring today. Now, the earth is heating up at a much faster pace than ever before. Scientists are becoming alarmed at the potentially catastrophic changes in climate that may be rapidly approaching.

For many years, influential climate scientists, such as Michael Mann, have been pointing out the danger of a possible runaway greenhouse effect on Earth. On the other hand, a small number of scientists, including Freeman Dyson and Nir Shariv, remain skeptical that human activity is influencing the climate. They believe that the climate is much too complex for scientists to create reliable models capable of predicting future changes in the climate, even using the most advanced computers.

EXCERPT FROM "TRANSCRIPT: UNDERSTANDING CLIMATE CHANGE: A CONVERSATION WITH MICHAEL MANN," FROM *THE BIG PICTURE WITH THOM HARTMANN* AND RT AMERICA, NOVEMBER 10, 2015

Thom Hartmann: Hello, I'm Thom Hartmann in Washington, D.C. and tonight we talk to one man for the hour, climate scientist Michael Mann in a special climate change edition of The Big Picture.

You need to know this: 100% of all credible climate scientists agree that global warming is real and that it's man-made. Some even think it's going to be a lot more destructive than we originally thought. So why is it taking so long to put together a comprehensive plan to stop climate change?

For the next hour we're going to delve into the details of global warming with world-renowned climate scientist Dr. Michael Mann. We'll go over the basics of what global warming is, what's causing it, we'll talk about some of the worse case scenarios involving runaway climate change, take down the denial myths pumped out by the fossil fuel industry and put forward solutions to the greatest environmental crisis our planet has seen perhaps in the history of the human race.

Joining me now from State College, Pennsylvania, is Dr. Michael Mann, distinguished professor of meteorology and director of the Earth System Science Center at Penn State University, and the author of the book *The Hockey Stick and the Climate Wars: Dispatches from the Front Lines*. Dr. Michael Mann, welcome back. It's great to have you with us.

Michael Mann: Thanks, Thom, it's great to be with you.

Thom Hartmann: Let's start off with the basics. Global warming is something most people have heard about, but probably even fewer actually understand. So, can you walk us through it in layman's language? What is global warming? Why is it happening? And perhaps most importantly, how do we know that it's happening?

Michael Mann: Sure. So, despite the fact that climate change, global warming, is sometimes characterized as new and controversial science, it's actually basic physics and chemistry that goes back nearly 2 centuries. And it has to do with the simple fact that certain gases in our atmosphere, like carbon dioxide, have this heat trapping ability - they keep some of the heat that comes in from the sun, warms the planet, some of the heat produced by the planet response is trapped within the atmosphere and so it warms up the planet to a higher temperature than it otherwise would be. In fact, if it were not for the greenhouse effect, we would live, or in fact we probably wouldn't be alive; Earth would be a frozen planet. So the greenhouse effect in fact is responsible for the fact that the Earth is a habitable planet. Of course, too much of a good thing can be a bad thing and in the case of fossil fuel burning and other human activities we are increasing the temperature of the Earth's surface by raising the greenhouse effect to an extent that we are already seeing some very damaging impacts.

Thom Hartmann: One of the biggest mistakes that people make when it comes to global warming or climate change is confusing weather with climate. Senator Jim Inhofe gave us a great example earlier this year. [Sen. James Inhofe (R-Okla.) entered the Senate carrying a snowball. He said, "In case we had forgotten, because we keep hearing that 2014 has been the warmest year on record, I ask the chair, do you know what this is? It's a snowball, just from outside here. So it's very, very cold out, very unseasonal. So here, Mr. President, catch this."]

Thom Hartmann: So, Dr. Mann, a lot of people are persuaded by that kind of stuff, it got heavy coverage on Fox so-called News. So walk us through this, what's the difference between climate and weather, and why could we have such a cold winter when the planet is warming so rapidly, at least the winter on the East Coast here?

Michael Mann: Right, so James Inhofe would do well to read some Mark Twain because Mark Twain explained this more than a century ago when he said that climate is what you expect, weather is what you get. Climate is the statistics of the weather. We can't predict what the exact weather will be here in State College two weeks from now, three weeks from now, let alone several years from now, but we can predict that six months from now it'll be colder and a year from now it will then be warmer again. That's seasonality. That's the seasonal cycle, and that's climate.

But climate is more than just the seasonal changes in temperature and rainfall patterns, it's the longer term changes due to things like El Niño events, due to natural factors like volcanoes and small but measurable changes in solar output, and of course due to human impacts, due to the increase in the concentration of these greenhouse gases from fossil fuel burning and other human activities.

So, what we know is that heat waves are becoming more common and will become more common and they'll become more intense. Hurricanes will become stronger. Sea level will continue to rise. We will see longer and more intense droughts over large parts of North America and other continents, and so on. Those are changes in the average statistics of the weather, and we know how they are going to change with some degree of confidence.

Thom Hartmann: You're the creator of the ...

Michael Mann: Now...

Thom Hartmann: Oh, I'm sorry, go ahead...

Michael Mann: Oh, I was just going to say, so it is true that we are seeing extreme weather events that we think are being impacted by climate change and sometimes the connection is a bit non-intuitive. For example, the very cold winters we've had in some parts of the eastern U.S. in recent years are part of an unusual change in the track of the jet stream. And that same track of the jet stream that's been bringing some unusually cold air plunging southward into the eastern U.S. has instead been bringing all the storms and the moisture with them up into Alaska, away from California, and that's part of why we are seeing record drought in California right now.

So, there are changes, for example, in the pattern of the jet stream that are giving us more extreme weather events of various sorts that we also think are related to climate change. We think that that change in the jet stream may be a result of the melting of sea ice up in the Arctic which actually changes the heating of the atmosphere, it changes the pattern of the jet stream. So there are various ways in which extreme weather events that are becoming more frequent, are probably as well tied to human-caused climate change.

Thom Hartmann: You're the creator of the famous hockey stick graph. What does that graph tell us about global warming and climate change?

Michael Mann: Well, it sort of reinforces what we already know. We know that the warming of the Earth is unusual; the warming that we've seen in recent decades, over the last century, and we know it's because of increasing green-house gas concentrations from human activity, from fossil fuel burning. What we didn't know for a long time was just how unusual is that sort of warming in a longer term context because we only have about a century or so of wide-spread thermometer measurements around the globe. So from the instrumental data alone we can only document how temperatures over the globe or temperatures in the northern hemisphere have changed over the past century or so. And that doesn't tell us how common it might be to see a warming trend of the magnitude we've seen over centennial time scales farther back into the past.

And so what we did back in the late 1990s was use information from what we call proxy records. These are indirect thermometers. They're things like tree rings and corals and ice cores and sediments, various physical or chemical measurements from our environment that actu-ally tell us something about past climate conditions. And we use those data to reconstruct how the temperature of the northern hemisphere had changed over the past thou-sand years.

And what we found was indeed that the recent warming has no precedent as far back as we were able to go. Now, since then, many other researchers using different methods, different types of data have independently sought to reconstruct climate back in time and we now know that the recent warming, the warming of the past few decades is likely without precedent even farther back. At least 1300 years, perhaps tens of thousands of years. Some of the work that has been done over the past few years suggests at least tentatively that we are now at a level of warming and a rate of warming that we cannot see going back into the last ice age and beyond.

Thom Hartmann: Wow. Outside of the pure data, what's the major evidence of global warming that we can see around us right now?

Michael Mann: Well, you know, we can see that ice is disappearing around the world, and it's doing so at an alarming rate. Mount Kilimanjaro, this magnificent ice-capped mountain at the equator, eastern equatorial Africa, immortalized by Ernest Hemingway's "Snows of Kilimanjaro", well those snows are disappearing before our eyes. We are seeing the loss of that ice cap and we know it's been around for more than 10,000 years.

We are seeing ice retreat around the globe. Sea ice, land ice, mountain glaciers, and the ice sheets; the Greenland ice sheets and the West Antarctic ice sheet. We are seeing rates of retreat of ice that have no precedent in tens of thousands of years. And that's really the cause for concern. It isn't just how warm we've made the planet, but the rate at which we are warming the planet, and the rate at which ice is disappearing, at which climate zones are migrating, climate change is occurring at a rate that is faster than we have reason to believe we or other living things can adapt to. It's really that rate, that dramatic rate of warming and of change in our climate. When human civilization developed over a period of relative climate stability and we depend on that climate stability. In fact, it's leveraged now by a population of more than 7 billion people and so we are highly dependent on the stability of our environment to support that very large population. And we're changing things faster than nature has changed them in the past. That's the cause for concern.

Thom Hartmann: How is global warming affecting or interacting with some of the major environmental crises we're seeing right now? California's drought, there are people suggesting that the whole Arab Spring phenomenon was the consequence of drought killing off the wheat crops in the Middle East, that sort of thing, in the minute that we have left in this block.

Michael Mann: Yeah, absolutely. One of the concerns here is that climate is what national security experts call a threat multiplier. It takes existing tensions over land, over water, over food and it exacerbates those tensions because it reduces access to food, land and water. And so it is sort of a perfect storm of consequences coming together to create potentially a major national security threat especially in regions like the Middle East which are already a tinder box. It's like adding fuel to the flame, climate change.

Thom Hartmann: Dr. Mann, one of the things I hear from right wingers all the time is that there actually hasn't been any warming over the last decade and a half. Is that true? And if not, where does this whole "pause in the warming" myth come from?

Michael Mann: Yes, one of what we call the climate change denial zombies. It doesn't matter how many times that myth, that talking point is disproven, is discredited, it just keeps on coming back. And there's absolutely no truth to the statement whatsoever. Every legitimate measurement of the temperature of the Earth, whether from satellites, whether from surface observations, thermometers, tells us that the globe continues to warm at a rate of about a degree Celsius per century. It's continuing on that trajectory as we expect it to. 2014 was the warmest year on record. 2015 is shaping up to be an even warmer year. 2015 is so far the warmest first half year that we've ever seen. So global warming continues apace. The globe continues to warm, ice continues to melt at an alarming level, but you continue to hear these specious claims that the globe isn't warming.

It in part comes from work that was done more than a decade ago which has now been entirely discredited. There was one group, two scientists, who are actually climate change contrarians and they had claimed for the longest time that the satellite data showed that the Earth wasn't warming when other scientists were able to get hold of that data, what they found was that those scientists had made what we call a sign error [sic]. What that means is that where there was supposed to be a plus in their algorithm, there was a minus sign. They were literally taking a warming trend and turning it into a cooling trend. And that work has now been exposed as invalid. Other scientists have gone in and done it the right way and the satellites show that the globe continues to warm at the rate we know it's warming from other lines of evidence.

Another example is what climate change contrarians will do, there's a sleight of hand in what they will often do: they will start with a very warm year like 1998. 1998 was the warmest year on record at that point, It was boosted by a big El Niño event [sic]; the warmest year that we had ever seen at that point. Now, of course, we have seen even warmer years. And what they'll do is they'll start their trend line with that very high 1998 value and then what they'll do is draw a trend line to subsequent years. Well, of course those subsequent years are cooler because you had just set a record in 1998. And so if you start playing those games, it's easy to distort what's actually happening through faulty statistics. And if you do it right, if you do it objectively, you stand back, you estimate the temperatures, the temperature trends correctly, what they show is that the globe continues to warm at the rate that climate models tell us it ought to be warming as we continue to pump these greenhouse gases into the atmosphere.

So, no matter how many times these talking points, these zombie climate change denier myths are struck down or discredited or refuted, they just keep coming back because there's a large audience for that sort of misinformation and disinformation, and often there isn't somebody there to correct the record when these specious claims are made.

Thom Hartmann: Tragically. The traditional benchmark for acceptable levels of global warming has been two degrees Celsius above preindustrial levels. Why that number, two degrees Celsius, and what happens after two degrees Celsius, and how close are we to reaching that benchmark?

Michael Mann: Yeah, well that's a great question. We often hold out that number two degrees Celsius, that's three and a half degrees Fahrenheit relative to pre-industrial times as that level of dangerous interference with the climate system. We've already warmed one degree Celsius. We've probably got at least another half a degree Celsius in the pipeline, just from the greenhouse gases we've put into the atmosphere so far. So that gives us a very small cushion, very little wiggle room. There's only about a half a degree Celsius left to play with before we exceed that two degrees Celsius warming threshold. And if we continue with business as usual—fossil fuel burning for another decade—then we will commit to passing that threshold. That's why it's so urgent to reduce our carbon emissions now.

Now, there is in reality no one fixed number, two degree Celsius. A lot of bad things we think happen if we warm the planet two degrees Celsius. But even worse things happen if we warm the planet three degrees Celsius, and so on. So rather than this being a cliff that we fall off at two degrees Celsius it's much more like a steadily sloping down hill and the further we go down that hill the more we imperil ourselves. But if we miss that two degrees Celsius exit, if we're unable to reduce our emissions rapidly enough to avoid that two degrees Celsius warming limit, it doesn't mean we give up, Thom. What it means is we take the next exit ramp. We take the 2.2 degree Celsius warming exit ramp. The less warming, the less likely it is that we will see dangerous and potentially irreversible changes in our climate.

But, you know, if you talk to people in Tuvalu, if you talk to people who inhabit low-lying island nations, if you talk to people who live in Miami Beach, if you talk to people who live in California, they'll tell you that dangerous climate change isn't some far-off thing that might happen in the future, it's happening now.

Thom Hartmann: Former NASA scientist James Hansen is saying that two degrees, that that two degree threshold is actually too high, that it allows for devastating multi meter high sea level rises. What do you think? And if Dr. Hansen is correct, what kind of consequences does that have for this whole process of how we're trying to stop global warming?

Michael Mann: well, you know, we dismiss what James Hansen has to say at our peril [sic]. He's often been criticized for making pronouncements like that but he has also shown a penchant for being remarkably prescient. Back in 1981 he published a groundbreaking paper that literally predicted how much warming we would see in the decades ahead with a remarkable degree of accuracy. Back in 1989 he spoke on the U.S. Senate floor, for the first a climate scientist said, you know, human caused climate change is here, we are seeing it. And he was right then. So he has this remarkable history of making prescient predictions about the future and what he's saying now should not be dismissed.

He is arguing for the possibility that we will see quite a bit more sea level rise, more melting from the ice sheets - the West Antarctic ice sheet, the Greenland ice sheet - than climate models currently predict. More rapid sea level rise over the next 50 years than the climate models predict. And in fact, if you look at the climate projections, if you look at the predictions we made about sea level rise, the predictions we've made about arctic sea ice and how fast it would decline, in many respects the climate is changing faster and with greater magnitude than we predicted just years ago.

And so it may very well be true that Hansen is right and the climate models that we are using right now upon which to base policy are actually underestimating the rate at which we will see rise in sea level and a whole array of other negative climate impacts. It really stresses the fact, what we call the precautionary principle. We are tampering with the only planet we know of in the universe that supports life. There is no planet B. If we screw this one up, there is no recourse. And so we should be extremely cautious in tinkering with a system we don't understand perfectly because the changes may end up being far worse than we predict today.

Thom Hartmann: Some scientists like Dr. Guy McPherson have an even bleaker view of global warming, say that it's making such drastic changes to the atmosphere that it's pushing us outside the habitable zone and that we might have already passed some irreversible tipping points [sic]. Here's a quick clip of Guy McPherson on that:

Guy McPherson: We're so close to the sun, we're so close to the inner edge of the habitable zone for life on Earth that even a minor change in atmospheric composition could push us out of the habitable zone. Well, we haven't made minor changes in the atmospheric chemistry of the Earth; we've made major changes in the atmospheric chemistry of the Earth.

Thom Hartmann: So, what do you think about that? Could global warming lead to the end of much or all life, at least all large and complex life on Earth?

Michael Mann: Well, I don't know about that. There's quite a bit of uncertainty about the projections and we always have to keep in mind worse case scenarios because, as I said before, the climate model projections have a history of actually having been too conservative. The scientific community, in a sense, has a history of having been too conservative. So, we shouldn't dismiss out of hand voices like James Hansen or even McPherson who are telling us that it could be worse than what the climate models are currently telling us.

That having been said, based on my assessment of the science, my objective assessment of what the science actually tells us right now, I don't think we've passed a tipping point yet where we go beyond the adaptive capacity of human civilization or beyond the adaptive capacity of living things. I don't think we've yet crossed that line. We have certainly committed to some dangerous changes in climate already and it's possible we have already warmed the oceans enough that they're going to melt the ice shelves around Antarctica enough to destabilize enough of that Antarctic ice to give us ten feet or eleven feet of sea level rise by the end of the century. That is a very real possibility.

And so there is some amount of adaptation that we are going to have to engage in. It isn't just a choice between mitigation—reducing our carbon emissions —and adaptation—taking measures to deal with the changes that are coming. We're going to have to do both.

But I think a sober look at what the science has to say, based for example on the most recently released report of the Intergovernmental Panel on Climate Change just a year or so ago. The best available science tells us it's not too late but there is an urgency unlike anything we've seen before. There is an urgency now to reduce our carbon emissions or we will potentially cross into what can only be described as the danger zone.

Thom Hartmann: How long before we might hit that danger zone? You wrote a piece for Scientific American suggesting just 2036 as I recall.

Michael Mann: Yeah. If we continue with business as usual, our carbon, burning of fossil fuels, with the growth of emissions in countries like China, India and South America, it's only a matter of a couple of decades before we cross that two degree Celsius warming and the science tells us a lot of bad things will happen with two degrees Celsius warming of the planet, but even worse things will happen with three degrees Celsius warming and far worse things with five degrees Celsius warming. And we are on track to exceed five degrees Celsius warming of the planet by the end of the century if we continue with business as usual. That's a larger change in global temperature than from the height of the last ice age when ice sheets covered New York to today.

We are talking abut a monumental change in climate on a time frame far shorter than anything that nature has ever produced before, and that's the real problem [sic]. We're talking about rates of change, magnitudes of change and rates of change that have no precedent in the past and may indeed, as some have speculated, lead to the sixth great extinction event. We are on course to the sixth great extinction event if we don't change our way of doing things.

Thom Hartmann: Dr. Mann, one of the things that concerns many scientists is the large stores of methane under the Arctic permafrost and under the Arctic Sea. There's actually more carbon apparently there under the surface of the Arctic than there is in the Earth's atmosphere. What happens if that carbon gets out and how could that happen?

Michael Mann: Yes, there was a study just last year that suggested that we could essentially double the warming from CO_2 alone, from carbon dioxide alone, from the potential release of some of this methane that's trapped in permafrost, that's trapped in the coastal shelves of the Arctic Ocean. And we can't rule out that scenario. It's a reminder that there is uncertainty. There are uncertainties, there are potential surprises that loom and they're not going to be pleasant surprises.

There are potential aggravating factors like the potential destabilization and release of methane that could make the problem worse than we currently project with our climate models. And so it once again highlights the fact that in many respects climate scientists have been overly conservative in the scenarios that we've envisioned and the changes that we've projected for the future. It could potentially be a whole lot worse. Now, there's a lot of uncertainty there and there is a fierce debate within carbon cycle scientists over just how much of that methane is potentially releasable into the atmosphere with the warming projected over the next century.

Some scientists say that only a fairly small part of that is mobile, can be mobilized by global warming, but some scientists think that potentially a much larger amount of that methane could be released. To the extent that there is uncertainty, it could once again break, not in our favor, but against us. And so, it's once again reason for precaution for not tampering any further with a system that we don't understand perfectly. And that's what we're doing. The distinguished climate scientist Wally Broeker of Columbia University once said it is like we are poking an angry beast with sticks. That's a dangerous thing to do, and that's what we're doing.

Thom Hartmann: This is the first time in this hour that we've mentioned methane. Can you just very quickly for viewers who might not understand why we suddenly went from talking about carbon dioxide to methane, what's the difference between carbon dioxide and methane and why should we be concerned about methane in the Arctic or anywhere else?

Michael Mann: Yes, methane, it turns out, is a more potent greenhouse gas than CO_2. A single methane molecule absorbs more atmospheric heating than a single CO_2 molecule. Now, there are other complications in comparing them, because methane has a different lifetime in the atmosphere. CO_2 stays around for a very long time. Methane tends to be absorbed by the climate system on a time frame of a decade or two decades and because of that it just doesn't stick around as much. And so when you are comparing the two problems you have to look at not just how much warming you can get, but the time scale over which that warming is likely to happen.

And it turns out that your metric of danger; what you think of and what you envision as dangerous climate change is going to determine to some extent the relative risks of these two contributors. If you are worried that we are going to pass some sort of tipping point within the next decade or two decades, where we trigger things like the dramatic acceleration of the melting of the ice sheets or the shutdown of the ocean circulation pattern that helps warm Europe, the conveyor belt ocean circulation, or a fundamental shift in the way that El Niño behaves that could have profound impacts for drought and rainfall patterns around the world, if you're worried abut those sorts of dramatic changes that could be triggered by an abrupt short term amount of warming, then methane, it turns out, is a real player. Methane really has the potential to aggravate the warming that we see over the next decade or two.

Now if you're worried about sort of the longer term warming of the planet, the longer term changes in climate, well then it's really CO_2 which is the main player. And so, to some extent, one's concern about CO_2 versus methane is going to depend on the things you're concerned about happening. What your tolerance is, what your metric is for defining dangerous changes in climate.

One would be best served by avoiding the increase in concentrations of both of them because they carry different types of risk as far as climate responses are concerned.

Now, methane is getting into the atmosphere a number of different ways. Methane is produced by livestock and by agriculture, so there's a certain amount of human-produced methane from agricultural practices, from livestock raising, but it's also escaping into the atmosphere because of fracking, because of natural gas drilling, the use of so-called fracking - hydraulic fracturing - to try to get at the methane, the natural gas that's contained in the bedrock below, where fluids are injected and they crack the bedrock and allow that methane to escape and potentially be recovered. But some of it actually escapes into the atmosphere. It's what we call fugitive methane.

And so the process of natural gas extraction and fracking, that's potentially introducing methane into the atmosphere. We don't know exactly how much. It could potentially offset the nominal gains from natural gas which is just a little less intensive from the greenhouse warming standpoint as burning coal. It doesn't produce quite as much CO_2 for the amount of energy that's generated. So some people have said well it's a natural gas, if we switch to natural gas from coal that can help lower our carbon emissions. But if a lot of that natural gas is actually escaping into the atmosphere, and that natural gas is mostly methane which is a very potent greenhouse gas, it could actually be making the problem even worse.

Then there is the natural gas, rather than methane, that is certainly trapped within the climate system, frozen in what is known as clathrate crystalline structure along the continental shelves of the oceans, the methane that is trapped in the permafrost. If we warm the planet up enough, we could, as we were discussing earlier, potentially release a lot of that, mobilize a lot of that methane and that again would add substantially to greenhouse warming.

So, it's a potentially important player and we have to be thinking not just about CO_2, but about other green-house gases that are being produced by human activity like methane.

Thom Hartmann: Moving on to climate denialism; how has this taken such a grip in America? Is it as prevalent in the rest of the world?

Michael Mann: Well, climate denialism to some extent has been manufactured. There is an ongoing decades-old industry-funded disinformation campaign to confuse the public about the science of climate change. So fossil fuel interests, and their abettors the Koch brothers, Koch Industries, other conservative interest groups have been spending tens of millions of dollars to pollute the larger public discourse over this issue by manufacturing contro-versy, by misrepresenting the science, by attacking the science and scientists in op-eds and through conserva-tive media outlets that have distorted the science of cli-mate change for their viewers. Fox News, the Wall Street Journal editorial pages, which is a fount of misinformation and disinformation when it comes to climate change [sic].

So that didn't just happen by accident. It happened because there was a well laid out well-financed strategy detailed decades ago to generate a fake debate about climate change to prevent action from occurring. To prevent the regulation of carbon emissions. Because those vested interests well knew that as long as they could maintain the appearance of controversy, the appearance that climate change is still debated by scientists, that would be enough to convince the public that we're not yet, that we don't have the degree of certainty necessary to act on this problem when ironically, if anything the uncertainty is breaking in the other direction. Things are potentially going to be even worse than what we have projected previously.

So, there has literally been this poisoning of the public discourse through tens of millions of dollars of special interest funding, of front groups. They hire fake experts with impressive credentials to attack their fellow scientists, to attack the science. They have created front groups which manufacture misinformation, which produce talking heads that go on television news programs, that write op-eds in leading newspapers, misleading the public about climate change. You see it here in the U.S. where there's a lot of fossil fuel money and there's a very large and powerful fossil fuel industry. You see it in Australia. You see it anywhere where there is a large vested interest that doesn't want to see the regulation of carbon emissions. You see these sorts of misinformation campaigns intended to distract the public and policymakers and lead them astray and prevent action from being taken.

Thom Hartmann: Well, and meanwhile, we see that, at least with television, for example, there's actually very little coverage of climate change. PBS beats CBS, ABC and NBC by almost 2 to 1 or maybe more than 2 to 1 last year in just even discussing the topics [sic]. Why do you think it is that Americans are so willing to accept that narrative of the climate deniers? Is it because there's so little coverage or is it because people just want a rosy outlook? Michael Mann: Yeah, I mean, I think it's a combination of factors. The fact is that many of these television news programs and many of the networks receive a lot of advertising money from fossil fuel interests. You can't watch any of the cable news networks without seeing multiple advertisements from the American Petroleum Institute, from ExxonMobil, sort of greenwash, where they present themselves as caring about the environment at the same time they are spending tens of millions of dollars sort of in misinformation, in perpetuating misinformation about climate change [sic]. The same time that they're hiring front groups to attack the science of climate change, sort of speaking out of both sides of their mouth. And so I think to some extent it has to do with biting the hand that feeds you. Many of these networks probably don't want to upset these corporate sponsors.

And so there hasn't been the sort of hard-hitting journalism, whether it's in the newspapers or whether it's on television, that there ought to be given the magnitude of the problem and the magnitude of the threat that it represents.

Thom Hartmann: Dr. Mann, we've put off dealing with this issue in any serious way for about 30 years that it's been fairly irrefutable. What needs to happen now to curb the worst outcome of climate change?

Michael Mann: Yeah, well as you say, we have unfortunately procrastinated in acting on this problem and there's a great procrastination penalty. If we had acted on the problem decades ago, when we had enough information already to know that climate change was real, that it was caused by human activity, that was going to increasingly be a threat, if we had acted then, then we would have been able to undergo a fairly slow and methodical transition away from fossil fuels towards renewable energy, to other forms of energy.

We could have undergone a slow enough transition that it could be accomplished fairly inexpensively. If you like, think of it, if you think of the carbon emissions, if we had brought them to a peak decades ago and had then gently brought them down in such a way as to avoid dangerous warming of the climate, the emissions curve would have looked like a bunny slope. Think of it as a bunny slope, OK.

Instead, by having delayed action, the peak is now much higher and we have to bring it down far more dramatically and far more quickly. So we've gone from the bunny slopes to the double diamond, the black double diamond slopes. That's the cost of not having acted on this problem sooner. And of course there's all the damage that has been done by climate change in the meantime.

So there has been a huge procrastination penalty in not have acting when we had enough information to act. That having been said, there is still time to act so that we avert the worst potential consequences of climate change. When we talked about the two degrees Celsius warming, three and a half degrees Fahrenheit warming, as being a warming threshold that we definitely want to avoid, beyond which we really start to see some of the bad things happen, we can still avoid crossing that two degree warming threshold, but it's going to take concerted action.

And what it's going to mean is that we have to very rapidly transition away from our current reliance on fossil fuels; on coal, on oil, on natural gas, and move towards solar energy, renewable energy, wind energy. We have the technology. The irony is that we don't have to invent new technologies to solve this problem. The technology already exists. We just have to scale it up.

And there is peer-reviewed work, some excellent work done by folks at Stanford University, Mark Jacobson and his group at Stanford University, that have shown that we have the technology, we have the ability to wean ourselves from fossil fuels by mid century, almost completely by mid century. And we have the ability to scale up solar and wind and other renewable sources of energy and they're doing it. It isn't just theoretical.

Germany is doing it. Germany is now meeting 30% of its energy demand from renewable energy alone.

We are seeing dramatic gains made to the point where for the first time in many decades last year we saw global economic growth without a growth in carbon emissions. There is now what appears to be taking place a decoupling of our economy from fossil fuels [sic]. We're starting to turn the corner but we have to turn that corner even faster. We really have to dramatically incentivize the shift away from fossil fuels. We've got to stop burning dirty coal. We've got to massively deploy renewable energy if we are going to avoid crossing those dangerous thresholds.

Thom Hartmann: You talked about, you kind of glanced off the economics of this. Let's talk about that. Fossil fuels receive massive subsidies world-wide, from the actual subsidies to fossil fuels, to subsidies like, you know, the American navy protecting our shipping lanes to get Saudi oil here. But renewables produce energy more cheaply when you consider those extra costs, and that's not even costing the externalities which I'd like you to address also. So what will it take to make the economics favorable for renewable energy to quickly overtake fossil fuels as a principle energy source around the world?

Michael Mann: Yeah, that's exactly right, and what we're seeing amazingly is that renewable energy is already making significant inroads in our energy economy even without those incentives. Imagine what we could be accomplishing right now if we put the proper incentives in place. Because right now we have an unequal playing field in the global energy market. We are, as you allude to, providing huge subsidies and incentives to the very form of energy, fossil fuel energy, which is destroying our climate; destroying, in some sense, our planet, and not providing similar incentives for the forms of energy, renewable energy, that can help us wean ourselves off of this dirty, dangerous fossil fuel energy.

So, the incentive structure right now is completely inverted from what it needs to be. I'm one of those people who thinks that the market can solve this problem. We can solve this problem in a market economy, through market mechanisms, but the playing field has to be leveled. And right now it's not level because we're providing incentives to the energy sources that are hurting the planet and not providing equal incentives to the energy sources that can help save the planet.

Now I saw just the other day that one of the Republican candidates for president Jeb Bush actually stated publicly that he thinks that we should do away with fossil fuel subsidies [sic]. And he was half right because he also said that we should do away with subsidies for renewable energy. And that's wrong. What we need to do is do away with the incentives for fossil fuel energy and incentivize the clean energy sources that can help us avert this potential catastrophe.

Thom Hartmann: Yeah, in fact, my understanding is that from news reports that the world wide subsidies for fossil fuels right now are around 5 trillion dollars a year. That would buy a lot of renewables.

At this point will we even know when we're seeing the worst outcomes or has erratic weather simply become the new normal?

Michael Mann: Yeah, the problem here is the variable tip of the iceberg, right. By the time you see the tip of the iceberg, it's too late. The Titanic learned that the hard way. And so it is with climate change. By the time you are able to see in the day to day weather, in the sorts of extremes that in daily weather, by the time the signal is so large that we are literally seeing it in the day to day weather, well then you know that we've gone too far already [sic]. You know that there's much more in the pipeline.

Because it is, to go back to that analogy, like the Titanic. The climate is this huge ship. It has huge amounts of inertia, what we call thermal inertia. The oceans can absorb a very large amount of heat so the climate system warms up fairly slowly, it's burying some of that heat below the surface. That's contributing towards global sea level rise, so it is this slow but steady warming that will persist for decades.

And in fact if we stopped burning carbon right now, not only would the surface of the Earth continue to warm for half a century, probably give us at least another half a degrees Celsius, but the oceans would continue to warm for centuries, and sea level rise will continue to rise for centuries [sic].

So, what that tells us is that we have already committed to a certain amount of additional and potentially dangerous changes in climate. We are going to need to adapt to those changes that are already locked in. There's a certain amount that's baked in, there's a certain amount of additional climate change that's baked in, that we are going to need to deal with, that we're going to need to find ways to adapt to the negative impacts of those climate changes that are already locked in. But we can still avoid the vast majority of climate change if we act now, the most dangerous and potentially irreversible changes in climate if we act now.

Thom Hartmann: This summer the Pope convened mayors from around the world to address what cities can do at the local level and small scale renewable energy is being deployed much more rapidly than large scale installations, at least from some reports I've seen. Is this how we have to address climate change, a grass roots bottom up approach?

Michael Mann: Yeah, and we see evidence of that here in the U.S. Right now we have, there's obviously intransigence in the U.S. Congress when it comes to passing meaningful comprehensive climate and energy legislation. We're just not going to see that as long as the politicians who were put in place by the Koch brothers in the last election through massive funding to put in place politicians who would be sympathetic to their agenda of climate change inaction [sic].

Obviously they now have a stranglehold on the U.S. House of Representatives and to some extent on the U.S. Senate as well. So in the absence of the potential for congressional legislation, what we need and are seeing is action at the Executive level. President Obama has pretty much done everything within his power to impose new carbon emissions limits on coal-fired power plants, increased fuel efficiency standards again through the EPA.

You see states banding together. And my friend Jerry Brown, the governor of California, is taking a lead role in seeing that California is at the leading edge of introducing a cost of carbon in their state economy so that carbon emissions are now going to be priced, again to start to internalize the damages done by the emission of carbon into the atmosphere.

And California is banding together with Oregon, Washington, and even British Columbia to institute a regional carbon emissions consortium. The northeastern states are doing something through what's known as RGGI, another regional carbon permit consortium are doing something as well [sic].

You see mayors passing measures at the local level, at the city level to do something about carbon emissions. The mayor of Los Angeles for example is leading that effort. Philadelphia, the mayor of Philadelphia, Michael Nutter, as well, as part of that effort among mayors of the major cities to do something to act on this problem in the absence of congressional leadership [sic].

And of course there was this very critical agreement that the president struck with China within the last year to make sure that the two largest nations, the two largest emitters of carbon on the face of the planet are engaged in efforts to bring down their carbon emissions.

Thom Hartmann: Dr. Michael Mann, it has been a pleasure and an honor talking to you. Thanks so much for being with us tonight.

Michael Mann: Thank you, it's been a pleasure to talk with you as well.

Thom Hartmann: And that's The Big Picture tonight. Don't forget, democracy begins with you. Get out there. Get active. Tag, you're it!

Transcribed by Sue Nethercott

1. Michael Mann mentioned that Mark Twain once explained that "climate is what you expect, but weather is what you get." What do you think Mark Twain meant by this?

2. What kinds of data do scientists use in order to reconstruct how the temperature of the northern hemisphere has changed over the past thousand years?

"LIMITED ROLE FOR CO$_2$," BY LAWRENCE SOLOMON, FROM *THE NATIONAL POST*

Astrophysicist Nir Shaviv, one of Israel's top young scientists, describes the logic that led him — and most everyone else — to conclude that SUVs, coal plants and other things man-made cause global warming.

Step One Scientists for decades have postulated that increases in carbon dioxide and other gases could lead to a greenhouse effect.

Step Two As if on cue, the temperature rose over the course of the 20th century while greenhouse gases proliferated due to human activities.

Step Three No other mechanism explains the warming. Without another candidate, greenhouses gases necessarily became the cause.

Dr. Shaviv, a prolific researcher who has made a name for himself assessing the movements of two-billion-year-old meteorites, no longer accepts this logic, or subscribes to these views. He has recanted: "Like many others, I was personally sure that CO2 is the bad culprit in the story of global warming. But after carefully digging into the evidence, I realized that things are far more complicated than the story sold to us by many climate scientists or the stories regurgitated by the media.

"In fact, there is much more than meets the eye."

Dr. Shaviv's digging led him to the surprising discovery that there is no concrete evidence — only speculation — that man-made greenhouse gases cause global warming. Even research from the Intergovernmental Panel on Climate Change— the United Nations agency that heads the worldwide effort to combat global warming — is bereft of anything here inspiring confidence. In fact, according to the IPCC's own findings, man's role is so uncertain that there is a strong possibility that we have been cooling, not warming, the Earth. Unfortunately, our tools are too crude to reveal what man's effect has been in the past, let alone predict how much warming or cooling we might cause in the future.

All we have on which to pin the blame on greenhouse gases, says Dr. Shaviv, is "incriminating circumstantial evidence," which explains why climate scientists speak in terms of finding "evidence of fingerprints." Circumstantial evidence might be a fine basis on which to justify reducing greenhouse gases, he adds, "without other 'suspects.'" However, Dr. Shaviv not only believes there are credible "other suspects," he believes that at least one provides a superior explanation for the 20th century's warming.

"Solar activity can explain a large part of the 20th-century global warming," he states, particularly because of the evidence that has been accumulating over the past decade of the strong relationship that cosmic-ray flux has on our atmosphere. So much evidence has by now been amassed, in fact, that "it is unlikely that [the solar climate link] does not exist."

The sun's strong role indicates that greenhouse gases can't have much of an influence on the climate — that CO_2 et al. don't dominate through some kind of leveraging effect that makes them especially potent drivers of climate change. The upshot of the Earth not being unduly sensitive to greenhouse gases is that neither increases nor cutbacks in future CO_2 emissions will matter much in terms of the climate.

Even doubling the amount of CO_2 by 2100, for example, "will not dramatically increase the global temperature," Dr. Shaviv states. Put another way: "Even if we halved the CO_2 output, and the CO_2 increase by 2100 would be, say, a 50% increase relative to today instead of a doubled amount, the expected reduction in the rise of global temperature would be less than 0.5C. This is not significant."

The evidence from astrophysicists and cosmologists in laboratories around the world, on the other hand, could well be significant. In his study of meteorites, published in the prestigious journal, Physical Review Letters, Dr. Shaviv found that the meteorites that Earth collected during its passage through the arms of the Milky Way sustained up to 10% more cosmic ray damage than others. That kind of cosmic ray variation, Dr. Shaviv believes, could alter global temperatures by as much as 15% —sufficient to turn the ice ages on or off and evidence of the extent to which cosmic forces influence Earth's climate.

In another study, directly relevant to today's climate controversy, Dr. Shaviv reconstructed the temperature on Earth over the past 550 million years to find that cosmic ray flux variations explain more than two-thirds of Earth's temperature variance, making it the most dominant climate driver over geological time scales. The study also found that an upper limit can be placed on the relative role of CO2 as a climate driver, meaning that a large fraction of the global warming witnessed over the past century could not be due to CO_2 — instead it is attributable to the increased solar activity.

CO_2 does play a role in climate, Dr. Shaviv believes, but a secondary role, one too small to preoccupy policy-makers. Yet Dr. Shaviv also believes fossil fuels should be controlled, not because of their adverse affects on climate but to curb pollution.

"I am therefore in favor of developing cheap alter-natives such as solar power, wind, and of course fusion reactors (converting Deuterium into Helium), which we should have in a few decades, but this is an altogether different issue." His conclusion: "I am quite sure Kyoto is not the right way to go."

Material republished with the express permission of: National Post, a division of Postmedia Network Inc.

1. Instead of increasing levels of CO_2 (carbon dioxide), what does Dr. Shaviv state is the cause of increased global warming?

"FREEMAN DYSON TAKES ON THE CLIMATE ESTABLISHMENT," BY MICHAEL D. LEMONICK, FROM *YALE ENVIRONMENT 360*, JUNE 4, 2009

Princeton physicist Freeman Dyson has been roundly criticized for insisting global warming is not an urgent problem, with many climate scientists dismissing him as woefully ill-informed. In an interview with Michael D. Lemonick, Dyson explains his iconoclastic views and why he believes they have stirred such controversy.

On March 3, *The New York Times Magazine* created a major flap in the climate-change community by running a cover story on the theoretical physicist Freeman Dyson that focused largely on his views of human-induced global warming.

Basically, he doesn't buy it. The climate models used to forecast what will happen as we continue to pump CO2 into the atmosphere are unreliable, Dyson claims, and so, therefore, are the projections. In an interview with *Yale Environment 360*, his first since the *Times* article appeared, Dyson contends that since carbon dioxide is good for plants, a warmer planet could be a very good thing. And if CO_2 does get to be a problem, Dyson believes we can just do some genetic engineering to create a new species of super-tree that can suck up the excess.

These sorts of arguments are advanced routinely by climate-change skeptics, and dismissed just as routinely by those who work in the field as clueless at best and deliberately misleading at worst. Dyson is harder to dismiss, though, in part because of his brilliance. He's on the faculty at the Institute for Advanced Study, where as a young physicist he hobnobbed with Albert Einstein. When Julian Schwinger, Sin-Itiro Tomonaga and Richard Feynman shared the 1965 Nobel Prize in physics for quantum electrodynamics, Dyson was widely acknowledged to be almost equally deserving — but the Nobel Committee only gives out three prizes for a given discovery.

Nevertheless, large numbers of climate modelers and others who actually work on climate change — as Dyson does not — rolled their collective eyes at assertions they consider appallingly ill-informed. In his interview with *Yale Environment 360*, Dyson also makes numerous assertions of fact — from his claim that warming today is largely confined to the Arctic to his contention that human activities are not primarily responsible for rising global temperatures — that climate scientists say are flat-out wrong.

Many climate scientists were especially distressed that the *Times* gave his views such prominence. Even worse, when the profile's author, Nicholas Dawidoff, was asked on NPR's "On The Media" whether it mattered if Dyson was right or wrong in his views, Dawidoff answered, "Oh, absolutely not. I don't care what he thinks. I have no investment in what he thinks. I'm just interested in how he thinks and the depth and the singularity of his point of view."

This is, to put it bluntly, bizarre. It matters a great deal whether he's right or wrong, given that his views have been trumpeted in such a prominent forum with essentially no challenge. So I visited Dyson in his Princeton office in May to probe a little deeper into his views on climate change.

Yale Environment 360: First of all, was that article substantially accurate about your views?

Freeman Dyson: It's difficult to say, "Yes" or "No." It was reasonably accurate on details, because they did send a fact-checker. So I was able to correct the worst mistakes.

But what I could not correct was the general emphasis of the thing. He had his agenda. Obviously he wanted to write a piece about global warming and I was just the instrument for that, and I am not so much interested in global warming. He portrayed me as sort of obsessed with the subject, which I am definitely not. To me it is a very small part of my life. I don't claim to be an expert. I never did. I simply find that a lot of these claims that experts are making are absurd. Not that I know better, but I know a few things. My objections to the global warming pro-paganda are not so much over the technical facts, about which I do not know much, but it's rather against the way those people behave and the kind of intolerance to criti-cism that a lot of them have. I think that's what upsets me.

e360: So it's a sense you get from the way the argument is conducted that it's not being done in an honest way.

Dyson: I think the difference between me and most of the experts is that I think I have a much wider view of the whole subject. I was involved in climate studies seriously about 30 years ago. That's how I got interested. There was an outfit called the Institute for Energy Analysis at Oak Ridge. I visited Oak Ridge many times, and worked with those people, and I thought they were excellent. And the beauty of it was that it was multi-disciplinary. There were experts not just on hydrodynamics of the atmosphere, which of course is important, but also experts on vegeta-tion, on soil, on trees, and so it was sort of half biological and half physics. And I felt that was a very good balance.

And there you got a very strong feeling for how uncertain the whole business is, that the five reservoirs of carbon all are in close contact — the atmosphere, the upper level of the ocean, the land vegetation, the topsoil, and the fossil fuels. They are all about equal in size. They all interact with each other strongly. So you can't understand any of them unless you understand all of them. Essentially that was the conclusion. It's a problem of very complicated ecology, and to isolate the atmosphere and the ocean just as a hydrodynamics problem makes no sense.

Thirty years ago, there was a sort of a political split between the Oak Ridge community, which included biology, and people who were doing these fluid dynamics models, which don't include biology. They got the lion's share of money and attention. And since then, this group of pure modeling experts has become dominant.

I got out of the field then. I didn't like the way it was going. It left me with a bad taste.

Syukuro Manabe, right here in Princeton, was the first person who did climate models with enhanced carbon dioxide and they were excellent models. And he used to say very firmly that these models are very good tools for understanding climate, but they are not good tools for predicting climate. I think that's absolutely right. They are models, but they don't pretend to be the real world. They are purely fluid dynamics. You can learn a lot from them, but you cannot learn what's going to happen 10 years from now.

What's wrong with the models. I mean, I haven't examined them in detail, (but) I know roughly what's in them. And the basic problem is that in the case of climate, very small structures, like clouds, dominate. And you cannot model them in any realistic way. They are far too small and too diverse.

So they say, 'We represent cloudiness by a parameter,' but I call it a fudge factor. So then you have a formula, which tells you if you have so much cloudiness and so much humidity, and so much temperature, and so much pressure, what will be the result... But if you are using it for a different climate, when you have twice as much carbon dioxide, there is no guarantee that that's right. There is no way to test it.

We know that plants do react very strongly to enhanced carbon dioxide. At Oak Ridge, they did lots of experiments with enhanced carbon dioxide and it has a drastic effect on plants because it is the main food source for the plants... So if you change the carbon dioxide drastically by a factor of two, the whole behavior of the plant is different. Anyway, that's so typical of the things they ignore. They are totally missing the biological side, which is probably more than half of the real system.

e360: Do you think it's because they don't consider it important, or they just don't know how to model it?

Dyson: Well, both. I mean it's a fact that they don't know how to model it. And the question is, how does it happen that they end up believing their models? But I have seen that happen in many fields. You sit in front of a computer screen for 10 years and you start to think of your model as being real. It is also true that the whole livelihood of all these people depends on people being scared. Really, just psychologically, it would be very difficult for them to come out and say, "Don't worry, there isn't a problem." It's sort of natural, since their whole life depends on it being a problem. I don't say that they're dishonest. But I think it's just a normal human reaction. It's true of the military also.

They always magnify the threat. Not because they are dishonest; they really believe that there is a threat and it is their job to take care of it. I think it's the same as the climate community, that they do in a way have a tremendous vested interest in the problem being taken more seriously than it is.

e360: When I wrote my first story about this in 1987, I had to say this is all theoretical, we haven't actually detected any signal of climate change. Now, people point to all sorts of signals, which are just the sort of things that were being predicted, based in part on the models. They made predictions and they've tested the predictions by seeing what happened in the real world, and they seem to be at least in the same direction, and in about the same magnitude, they were predicting. So isn't that a hint that there is something right about the models?

Dyson: Of course. No doubt that warming is happening. I don't think it is correct to say "global," but certainly warming is happening. I have been to Greenland a year ago and saw it for myself. And that's where the warming is most extreme. And it's spectacular, no doubt about it. And glaciers are shrinking and so on.

But, there are all sorts of things that are not said, which decreases my feeling of alarm. First of all, the people in Greenland love it. They tell you it's made their lives a lot easier. They hope it continues. I am not saying none of these consequences are happening. I am just questioning whether they are harmful.

There's a lot made out of the people who died in heat waves. And there is no doubt that we have heat waves and people die. What they don't say is actually five times as many people die of cold in winters as die of heat in summer. And it is also true that more of the warming happens in winter than in summer. So, if anything, it's heavily favorable as far as that goes. It certainly saves more lives in winter than it costs in summer.

So that kind of argument is never made. And I see a systematic bias in the way things are reported. Anything that looks bad is reported, and anything that looks good is not reported.

A lot of these things are not anything to do with human activities. Take the shrinking of glaciers, which certainly has been going on for 300 years and has been well documented. So it certainly wasn't due to human activities, most of the time. There's been a very strong warming, in fact, ever since the Little Ice Age, which was most intense in the 17th century. That certainly was not due to human activity.

And the most serious of almost all the problems is the rising sea level. But there again, we have no evidence that this is due to climate change. A good deal of evidence says it's not. I mean, we know that that's been going on for 12,000 years, and there's very doubtful arguments as to what's been happening in the last 50 years and (whether) human activities have been important. It's not clear whether it's been accelerating or not. But certainly, most of it is not due to human activities. So it would be a shame if we've made huge efforts to stop global warming and the sea continued to rise. That would be a tragedy. Sea level is a real problem, but we should be attacking it directly and not attacking the wrong problem.

e360: Another criticism that's been leveled is that your thoughts and predictions about the climate models are relatively unsophisticated, because you haven't been in close contact with the people who are doing them. But if you sit down and actually talk to the people about what goes into the models today and what they are thinking about and how they think about clouds, you might discover that your assumptions about what they are doing are not correct. Is that plausible? Do you think it might inform you better to actually sit down with these people and find out what they are doing today?

Dyson: Well, it depends on what you mean by sitting down with people. I do sit down with people. I don't go over their calculations in detail. But I think I understand pretty well the world they live in.

I guess one thing I don't want to do is to spend all my time arguing this business. I mean, I am not the person to do that. I have two great disadvantages. First of all, I am 85 years old. Obviously, I'm an old fuddy-duddy. So, I have no credibility.

And, secondly, I am not an expert, and that's not going to change. I am not going to make myself an expert. What I do think I have is a better judgment, maybe because I have lived a bit longer, and maybe because I've done other things. So I am fairly confident about my judgment, and I doubt whether that will change. But I am certainly willing to change my mind about details. And if they find any real evidence that global warming is doing harm, I would be impressed. That's the crucial point: I don't see the evidence...

And why should you imagine that the climate of the 18th century — what they call the preindustrial climate — is somehow the best possible?

e360: I don't think people actually believe that. I think they believe it's the one during which our modern civilization arose. And that a rapid change to a different set of circumstances wouldn't be worse in a grand sense, but it would be very badly suited to the infrastructure that we have got.

Dyson: That's sort of what I would call part of the propaganda — to take for granted that any change is bad.

e360: It's more that any change is disruptive. You don't think that's reasonable?

Dyson: Well, disruptive is not the same as bad. A lot of disruptive things actually are good. That's the point. There's this sort of mindset that assumes any change is bad. You can call it disruptive or you can call it change. But it doesn't have to be bad.

e360: One thing is that if the temperature change projections are accurate for the next 100 years, it would be equivalent to the change that took us out of the last Ice Age into the present interglacial period, which is a very dramatic change.

Dyson: Yes, that's highly unlikely. But it's possible certainly.

e360: And the further argument is that this would happen much more quickly than that change happened. So it is hard to imagine that, at least in the short run, it could be anything but highly destructive.

Dyson: There's hidden assumptions there, which I question, that you can describe the climate by a single number. In the case of the Ice Age, that might be true, that it was cold everywhere. The ice was only in the northern regions, but it was also much colder at the equator in the Ice Age.

That's not true of this change in temperature today. The change that's now going on is very strongly concentrated in the Arctic. In fact in three respects, it's not global, which I think is very important. First of all, it is mainly in the Arctic. Secondly, it's mainly in the winter rather than summer. And thirdly, it's mainly in the night rather than at the daytime. In all three respects, the warming is happening where it is cold, not where it is hot.

e360: So, the idea is that the parts that are being disrupted are the parts that are inhospitable to begin with?

Dyson: Mostly. It is not 100 percent. But mostly they are, Greenland being a great example.

e360: Do you mind being thrust in the limelight of talking about this when it is not your main interest. You've suddenly become the poster child for global warming skepticism.

Dyson: Yes, it is definitely a tactical mistake to use somebody like me for that job, because I am so easily shot down. I'd much rather the job would be done by some-body who is young and a real expert. But unfortunately, those people don't come forward.

e360: Are there people who are knowledgeable about this topic who could do the job of pointing out what you see as the flaws?

Dyson: I am sure there are. But I don't know who they are. I have a lot of friends who think the same way I do. But I am sorry to say that most of them are old, and most of them are not experts. My views are very widely shared.

Anyway, the ideal protagonist I am still looking for. So the answer to your question is, I will do the job if nobody else shows up, but I regard it as a duty rather than as a pleasure.

e360: Because it is important for you that people not take drastic actions about a problem that you are not con-vinced exists?

Dyson: Yes. And I feel very strongly that China and India getting rich is the most important thing that's going on in the world at present. That's a real revolution, that the cen-ter of gravity of the whole population of the world would be middle class, and that's a wonderful thing to happen. It would be a shame if we persuade them to stop that just for the sake of a problem that's not that serious.

And I'm happy every time I see that the Chinese and Indians make a strong statement about going ahead with burning coal. Because that's what it really depends on, is coal. They can't do without coal. We could, but they certainly can't.

So I think it is very important that they should not be under pressure. Luckily they are, in fact, pretty self-confident; (neither) of those countries pays too much attention to us.

But that's my motivation... Anyhow, I think we have probably said enough.

1. Why doesn't Freeman Dyson believe that human activity is causing global warming?

2. If the Earth is actually warming, why does Dyson think this would be a good thing?

CHAPTER 3

WHAT CLIMATE ACTIVISTS SAY

In December 2015, COP21 took place in Paris, France. Since 1979, the nations of the world had been holding meetings to address the complex problems arising from climate change. The goal was always to try to come to an agreement to slow the pace of global warming. In spite of these efforts, the world continued to heat up, with 2015 being the warmest year on record. In Paris, the representatives of more than 190 nations finally reached an agreement to slow global warming by curbing greenhouse gas emissions. The agreement set a long-term goal of keeping global warming "well below" 2 degrees Celsius (3.6 degrees Fahrenheit) and working toward limiting the temperature rise to 1.5 degrees Celsius (2.7 degrees Fahrenheit).

To reach the designated target, the world's governments pledged to set national targets limiting emissions "as soon as possible." Many people around the world were encouraged that the agreement had been reached. But because the agreement stopped short of setting specific targets, many environmentalists and climate activists were disappointed. For some activists, it was clear that a long, difficult struggle would still be necessary to arrive at an agreement that mandated specific amounts of emissions reductions for each country if catastrophic global warming is to be prevented.

Other activists have been vocal about the role that large gas companies like ExxonMobil have in global warming and have actively tried to petition the US government to pursue charges against this corporation. In our last selection, a climate activist attempts to understand the "other side" of the debate.

"THE PARIS CLIMATE TALKS AND THE 1.5C TARGET: WARTIME-SCALE MOBILIZATION IS OUR ONLY OPTION LEFT," BY MARGARET KLEIN SALAMON AND EZRA SILK, FROM COMMON DREAMS, DECEMBER 16, 2015

The Paris climate talks are over, and the postmortems on the final agreement are flooding in. Here's our take:

After 21 years of negotiations, we finally have an agreement that the majority of nations are expected to ratify. This is a critical breakthrough in terms of shared global understanding of the crisis.

We are grateful that world leaders have agreed to make an effort to collectively tackle the climate crisis.

However, we are disturbed that it has taken this long, and that the agreement is not even close to strong enough to effectively protect civilization and the natural world.

We are glad that, now that an agreement has been reached, the climate movement can focus on national action — getting individual countries to race to zero emissions at wartime speed.

We're also glad that the 2°C heat limit target has at last been exposed as exceedingly immoral and dangerous in the mass media. We are grateful that the world community has signed onto language aiming to keep temperatures "well below" 2°C.

We're seriously concerned, however, that a new narrative is emerging portraying 1.5°C of warming as relatively "safe." The fact is that the earth is already dangerously too hot at current warming of 1°C – which is higher than human civilization has ever experienced. The truth is that all further global warming is extremely dangerous. We have no carbon budget left to burn.

Climate science tells us that the current level of greenhouse gases in the atmosphere is enough to eventually produce at least 2°C of warming. That's why we need an all-hands-on-deck effort to reduce atmospheric greenhouse gas concentrations as quickly as possible.

Ultimately, the Paris Agreement's target of global net zero greenhouse gas emissions in "the second half of this century" represents a cataclysmic failure of leadership — and likely a crime against humanity and the natural world — that will devastate the planet and civilization if it is realized.

We believe humanity can still prevent civilization-destroying global warming — but only if we undertake a WWII-scale Mobilization to restore a safe climate immediately. We need to transition off of fossil fuels and carbon-intensive agriculture as soon as humanly possible. That means an emergency restructuring of the entire economy at wartime speed to achieve net zero emissions in the U.S. by 2025, net zero emissions globally by 2030, as well as an urgent effort to draw down the excess carbon dioxide that has accumulated in the atmosphere since the Industrial Revolution.

That is the expressed goal of our organization, The Climate Mobilization. Our tool is The Pledge to Mobilize, which calls for this Mobilization, and can be signed by every person on the planet, both citizens and politicians alike.

Unfortunately, President Obama and American climate negotiators at the Paris talks did not heed our open letter calling on them to champion a Mobilization that drives the U.S. economy to zero emissions by 2025 at the Paris talks. The letter, which was written by our advisor, Tom Weis, was signed by over 1,400 people, including Mark Ruffalo, IPCC coordinating lead author Ove Hoegh-Guldberg, Ed Begley, Jr., Lester Brown, Terry Tempest Williams, Josh Fox, David Suzuki, Tim DeChristopher, Yeb Saño, the founder of the Woods Hole Research Center, the founder of the New Evangelical Partnership for the Common Good, and the former secretary of the California Environmental Protection Agency.

However, there are heartening signs that the public discussion is turning toward the need for a lightning-fast mobilization of the economy.

In *The Guardian* Sunday, Bill McKibben characterized the pace of the transition as "the only important question" in the wake of the Paris talks: "Our only hope is to decisively pick up the pace. In fact, pace is now the key word for climate...We know where we're going now; no one can doubt that the fossil fuel age has finally begun to wane, and that the sun is now shining on, well, solar. But the question, the only important question, is: how fast."

Attempting to answer that question in a fantastic front page piece for *The New York Times*, climate change reporter Justin Gillis interviewed scientists and found that a target of zero emissions globally by 2030 could potentially limit global warming to 1.5°C:

"A serious campaign to meet the more ambitious goal would mean that in less than two decades, the nations of the world would likely have to bring an end to gasoline cars, to coal- or gas-burning power plants in their current form, and to planes or ships powered by fossil fuels."

Climate scientist Glenn Peters has projected that meeting the 1.5C heat limit would require a global fossil fuel phase-out between 2025 and 2030, as well as a large-scale effort to remove excess carbon dioxide from the atmosphere.

Similarly, a group of scientists writing in *The Hindu* found that developed countries such as the U.S. would need to reach zero emissions in "the next 5-10 years" for a 50 to 66 percent chance of limiting warming to 1.5°C. Those aren't very good odds, either!

There is no conceivable way to achieve such a quick transition to zero emissions only using market-based mechanisms such as carbon pricing. Only a wartime-style mobilization, in which government regulation mandates the early retirement or conversion to zero emissions of all greenhouse-gas emitting plant and equipment, could possibly facilitate such drastic changes on such a tight time-frame without crashing the economy.

In fact, that's exactly what Gillis concluded in a Dec. 15, 2014 news analysis, in which he wrote that the only conceivable way to stabilize temperatures even lower than the now discredited 2°C "guardrail" would be through either "a technological miracle, or a mobilization of society on a scale unprecedented in peacetime."

We are not aware of any other campaign calling for zero emissions by 2025 in the U.S. or zero emissions globally by 2030 through a wartime-style mobilization. Unless we have missed something, The Climate Mobilization is literally the only campaign on earth calling for action that has a chance of saving our climate and our civilization. Don't take it from us – just pick up *The New York Times*!

Iowa Mobilizer Ed Fallon has asked Democratic Presidential candidates Bernie Sanders, Hillary Clinton, and Martin O'Malley to sign the Pledge to Mobilize multiple times (click on the links to see video), and none have signed so far. Now that the growing discussion of the 1.5°C target has demonstrated the immense urgency of our situation, we hope they each take another look at the Pledge, and consider championing a full-scale Climate Mobilization.

Fortunately, there are already several plans in existence describing how the climate mobilization we need to save civilization can work. Here are three that we highly recommend:

- *The One Degree War Plan*, by Paul Gilding and Jorgen Randers
- *Striking Targets*, by Philip Sutton
- *Plan B 4.0: Mobilizing to Save Civilization*, by Lester Brown

Please consider getting more involved in this campaign. Join us on a Thursday night organizing call. Take another look at our manifesto, "The Transformative Power of Climate Truth." Start a campaign for Climate Mobilization in your congressional district by sending our modifiable cover letter & executive summary to your congressional representative. Support our work with a donation.

We need to turn this into an enormous grassroots movement, and we need to do it quickly. We need to bring the rest of the environmental movement and the American people on board with the call for Climate Mobilization NOW! If we succeed, we will be heroes.

1. Do you think that Climate Mobilization is a good idea? Why or why not? Would you be willing to sign the pledge to mobilize?

2. What would the nations of the world have to do in order to reach zero emissions and limit global warming to 1.5°C by 2030?

"SEETHING WITH ANGER, PROBE DEMANDED INTO EXXON'S UNPARALLELED CLIMATE CRIME," BY JON QUEALLY, FROM COMMON DREAMS, OCTOBER 30, 2015

A broad coalition of community groups along with prominent leaders from the nation's top civil rights, environmental, and indigenous people's movements on Friday sent a joint letter to the U.S. Department of Justice demanding a federal investigation into allegations that oil giant ExxonMobil knew about the role fossil fuels played in driving climate change since the 1970s but concealed that information—and later sought to discredit those issuing warnings—in order to protect its own financial interests.

Addressed to Attorney General Loretta Lynch, the letter cites recent reporting by the *Los Angeles Times* and *Inside Climate News*—both of which offered devastating details into the manner and scope of the decades-long public deceit—and argues that a DOJ probe is warranted to determine whether criminal charges should be brought against the energy behemoth.

Given the damage that has already occurred from climate change—particularly in the poorest communities of our nation and our planet—and that will certainly occur going forward, these revelations should be viewed with the utmost apprehension," the letter states. "They are reminiscent—though potentially much greater in scale—than similar revelations about the tobacco industry."

Kicked off by the investigative reporting and spearheaded by 350.org co-founder Bill McKibben—who staged a one-person civil disobedience action earlier this month to draw attention to the issue—the call for a federal investigation has been growing over recent weeks.

"Despite Exxon's wealth and power, people were eager to sign on to this statement," McKibben said on Friday. "Anyone who's lived through 25 years of phony climate debate, or who's seen the toll climate change is already taking on the most vulnerable communities, has been seething at these revelations. It reminds me of the spirit at the start of the Keystone battle."

Just over two weeks ago, U.S. Reps. from California Ted Lieu (D-Los Angeles) and Mark DeSaulnier (D-Walnut Creek) also wrote a letter to Lynch demanding an investigation and specifically called for RICO statutes to be used to determine whether or not the behavior of Exxon constituted a criminal conspiracy.

"If these allegations against Exxon are true, then Exxon's actions were immoral," Lieu and DeSaulnier wrote to the attorney general. "We request the DOJ investigate whether ExxonMobil's actions were also illegal."

Initiating a public petition campaign to bolster their call for the DOJ probe, McKibben sent a letter to members of 350.org on Friday morning in which he stated "very few things truly piss me off," but that in his mind it seems that no corporation has ever "done anything bigger and badder" than what ExxonMobil has done in this case.

"Just think how much would be different if Exxon had told the truth," he continued. "We wouldn't fully have solved global warming but we'd be well on the way—there would have been no 25 year phony pretend debate. There'd be a lot more solar panels, and a lot less carbon in the air. There'd be a lot more green jobs, and a lot fewer communities, most of them low income and communities of color, dealing with the terrible health impacts of pollution. None of you would have had to fight simply to get climate change taken seriously; instead we'd all be hard at work on solutions."

That, of course, is not how the last four decades have played out and for that, he stated, "I think we should be angry."

The full text of Friday's letter and list of signatories follows:

Dear Attorney General Lynch,

As leaders of some of the nation's environmental, indigenous peoples and civil rights groups, we're writing to ask that you initiate a federal probe into the conduct of ExxonMobil. New revelations in the Los Angeles Times and the Pulitzer-prize-winning InsideClimate News strongly suggest that the corporation knew about the dangers of climate change even as it funded efforts at climate denial and systematically misled the public.

Given the damage that has already occurred from climate change—particularly in the poorest communities of our nation and our planet—and that will certainly occur going forward, these revelations should be viewed with the utmost apprehension. They are reminiscent—though potentially much greater in scale—than similar revelations about the tobacco industry.

These journalists have provided a remarkable roadmap to this corporation's potential misconduct. We would ask that you follow that map wherever it may lead, employing all the tools at your disposal to uncover the truth.

Signed,
Margie Alt, Executive Director of Environment America
Kenny Ausubel, Nina Simons, Founders of Bioneers
Sally Bingham, President and Founder of Interfaith Power and Light
May Boeve, Bill McKibben, Founders of 350.org
Michael Brune, Executive Director of Sierra Club
Robert Bullard, Author and John Muir Award winner, 2013
Andrea Carmen, Executive Director of International Indian Treaty Council
Faith Gemmill, Executive Director of REDOIL (Resisting Environmental Destruction on Indigenous Lands)
Tom Goldtooth, Executive Director of Indigenous Environmental Network
James Hansen, Director, Climate Science, Awareness and Solutions Program, Columbia University Earth Institute
Reverend Fletcher Harper, Executive Director of Greenfaith
David Helvarg, Executive Director of Blue Frontier
Gene Karpinski, President of League of Conservation Voters
Jane Kleeb, Bold Nebraska
Steve Kretzmann, Executive Director and Founder of Oil Change International
Fred Krupp, President of Environmental Defense Fund
Winona LaDuke, Executive Director of Honor the Earth
Annie Leonard, Executive Director of Greenpeace USA
RL Miller, President of Climate Hawks Vote
Matt Nelson, Managing Director of Presente.org
Brant Olson, Campaign Director at Climate Truth
Erich Pica, President of Friends of the Earth
Cindy Shogan, Executive Director of Alaska Wilderness League
Reverend Fred Small, President of Creation Coalition

Gus Speth, Former Dean Yale School of Forestry and the Environment
Tom Steyer, Founder of NextGen
Rhea Suh, President of the Natural Resources Defense Council
Vien Truong, Director of Green for All
Joe Uehlein, Executive Director of Labor Network for Sustainability
Tripp Van Noppen, President of Earthjustice
David Yarnold, President of the Audubon Society
Reverend Lennox Yearwood, President of Hip Hop Caucus
Trip Van Nopen, Earth Justice
Rich Stolz, Executive Director of OneAmerica
Resilience Collaborative, LLC
A Philip Randolph Institute
Green America
Energy Action Coalition
Divest Invest Individual
Bean Soup Times
Ecumenical Poverty Initiative
Beats Rhymes & Relief
Freddie Gray Project
Beloved Community Center
Neighbors United of Southeast Greensboro, NC
The Foundation of Women in Hip Hop
The Gathering for Justice/Justice League NYC
J Dilla Foundation
J.A.M.N.

that revelations that the company knew about climate change as early as the 1970s, but chose to mislead the public about the crisis in order to maximize their profits from fossil fuels.

1. Would you sign a letter advocating for a federal probe into Exxon's actions regarding climate change? Why or why not?

"US AND THEM: ON UNDERSTANDING CLIMATE DENIALISM," BY MARTIN KIRK, FROM COMMON DREAMS, MARCH 19, 2015

So we're in the midst of another round of climate-change related mud slinging. The latest issue of *National Geographic*, "The War on Science", was seen to sneer at the 130 million American who don't believe in human induced climate change. *The Washington Times'* Stephen Moore fired back with an emotional op-ed titled "The Myth of Settled Science," and to go by the pundits and the comment threads, people on both sides are tearing their hair out, utterly sick of what they see as their opponents' brainwashed, dangerous nonsense.

I get it. I feel it. But there are quieter moments when I just want to understand what's really going on. It's all too easy to fall into the trap of thinking all of those 130 million people who question the evidence must, at this point in the game, be either willfully uninformed or just stupid, but I know the real stupidity is in thinking that can be the case. So instead of presuming fault or failure, how does this debate look if we assume they are logical, have integrity, and are smart?

Here are two explanations for climate denialism that seem to me to hold water.

1. LEVELS OF REALITY

One thing that has been particularly confusing is how the political right managed to convince conservative Christians to reject so much evidence about the wholesale disrespect for, and destruction of, God's glorious creation. It seems to me that at least some of the answer for this lies in confusion, on both sides, between the idea of science as a method, and what the theologian Huston Smith calls "scientism."

The scientific method, in this context, is a process for studying reality made up of matter and energy. That's what it does, and that's all it does. Which is an immense and never-ending task, of course, but it is still contained within the box of objective physical reality. This why it can get no further back than the Big Bang. As the astrophysics David Schramm put it, "The universe did not necessarily begin with the big bang . . . Our universe, however, did, since we can obtain no information about the events that occurred before it." Put another way, the absence of evidence is not evidence of absence. The scientific method has nothing to offer reality that is not material or objective. It has nothing to say about values, in their final and proper sense (the very pursuit of knowledge, for example, is a value we've long assumed that is not, in fact, scientifically derived), or life meaning, and it is strictly mute on concepts of God.

Scientism, on the other hand, says that because matter and energy are all that the scientific method can measure, that's all there can be. Absence of evidence is evidence of absence. This leads to the basic premise that we, with our tools of perception and level of consciousness, are able to find all the answers and understand everything.

One is a method of investigation, the other is about as deep an ontological statement as can be. One is mute on questions of God, the other denies, even derides the very idea.

At the foghorn level of public debate all nuance is lost, of course, which is how this descends into a battle between Science in the one corner, and Religion in the other. And the fires have been stoked in this way for so long that both sides feel the debate is now a profound battle for Truth, which is the worst possible frame for finding common ground. We will never be able to work together if Absolute Truth is what we are fighting over, because none of us has access to it. Simply by virtue of being human, we all rely on a subjective mish-mash of experience, social influences, philosophy, theology, politics etc. It is the greatest unsettled, and objectively unsettle-able theme in all of human history. The sun will die and obliterate the Earth before we agree.

The liberal left, with our uber-rationalist instincts, activate this frame every time we say something like, "Well, Science says... ." *The National Geographic* piece is a good example of this, and it's nonsense. Science can't speak, any more than cooking, or philosophy, or practicing the piano can speak. It is a method. Only evidence speaks. I know that's what is meant in many cases, but the short-hand has been allowed to assume an ideological identity in its own right, easily – and sometimes correctly – heard as God-mocking Scientism. The minute you activate this frame, you hand power to the small number of rabid extremists who are genuinely uninterested in anything but their own image, wealth and power and will happily bully and deceive to get their way.

And the conservative Christian right has all too often bought into the simplistic hype that everyone who talks about the evidence of climate change must represent scientism on the march; an army of cold hearted atheists, spitting on their experience of reality beyond the material. When really, most of us, in my long experience, are not interested in presenting the scientific method as an all-knowing ontological force, nor would we countenance such disrespect. False battle-lines all over the map.

If we assume that we share the intention to live honestly and be guided by love and empathy, we are freed from the toxic rivers of anger and recrimination. We can acknowledge this shared intent, agree what we're talking about – a specific set of objective evidence – and leave the ontological debate for another time.

2. LONG TERM STRATEGY

OK, that might help me understand the instinct of some well-intentioned conservative Christians, but what's driving the good people of the political right?

For this, the most compelling theories come from two sources. The first is Naomi Klein. I think she has it right when she says, in her recent book *This Changes Everything* that the right, far from being slow and regressive, were actually a lot quicker off the mark than the left. They recognized from the get-go that climate change presents a wholesale challenge to what they believe to be the most positive economic system ever created: capitalism. If you believe it is a deeply positive force, then it makes perfect sense that you respond to a threat to capitalism as a threat to human progress and wellbeing.

That could account for an initial instinct, but surely not a long-term strategy. At some point it becomes self-defeating, right?

The next piece of the puzzle comes from the economist Philip. E. Mirowski. He suggests – pretty convincingly, to my ears - that the right has a perfectly coherent strategy for mitigating the threat of climate change, and it isn't just to ignore it so they can keep hoarding wealth while everyone else suffers, like so many Scrooge McDucks.

Stage One is to deny and cast doubt on the evidence. The thing to acknowledge about this is that it is a delaying tactic, not a statement of belief. It's based on the logic that if the threat is widely perceived too quickly, the most likely outcome is a knee-jerk response driven by panic and irrationality that could very well destroy all the good with the bad. Doctors would call this an iatrogenic effect – when the medicine causes more harm than the original disease.

Stage Two, once outright denial starts to lose its power, is to promote tepid market-based 'solutions,' like Cap and Trade, or the United Nation's REDD program, which aims to put a market price on rain forests, grasslands and the like, ostensibly to protect them. Again, these aren't believed to be full solutions, but they are useful for three reasons. Firstly, they promote the idea of 'free market' capitalism as a guiding economic model, so are both good long-term strategic messages, and easy to rally the broad tent of Right, and even plenty of left-of center players (many large NGOs, like WWF, actively support UN REDD). Secondly, they may actually help slow the onset of the threat; plenty of studies and a certain type of intuitive logic can be called on to validate this claim. And thirdly, and most importantly, it buys more time.

Stage Three is when the real solution comes in to play: unleash the full power of market-driven technology on the problem. Specifically, geoengineering. We needed Stages One and Two because of the time needed for this to become even remotely viable. We're talking about technologies capable of re-balancing the entire Earth's atmosphere; things like reflective aerosols in the atmosphere; modifying weather patterns through cloud seeding; and even building a giant sunshade in space. These things still sound quite a way out there to most, and none is proven at scale, which is why none is being actively championed just yet, but you can either see that as that there are no such solutions, or that there are no such solutions yet.

Agree or disagree with the thinking all you like (I certainly find it cut-through with inconsistencies and logical holes), but consider for a moment how smart it is. For a start, it's wrapped in a more sophisticated analysis not just of facts and figures, but social and political psychology, than anything the left has managed. We're still only now, and slowly, learning that doomsday scenarios are not a reliable motivator. It also works with the values and machinery of the economic system they subscribe to: materialism, market forces, and technological innovation. And finally, it is actually a rather elegant and complete long-term strategy. Again, something the left has yet to get together on. We're essentially still relying on brute rationalism to win the day. And we're losing. Or, at best and on a hopeful day, not winning anywhere close to fast enough.

If this is the strategy – which is a big if, but assuming it is roughly in the right area – then it isn't the "give us everything and damn the rest of you" horror show of the caricatures. And that means there is space in there for common ground, if only, to begin with, on the most basic idea that we must find the best way to protect this planet and the life on it.

From there I can say, free from anger and hopefully in tones that allow me to be heard by the good people on the other side, I respect your beliefs and I share your intent. We agree this world is precious, and life everywhere matters. That, to me, sounds like an important step closer to being able to work together than, "I think you are brainwashed and dangerous."

1. What do you think about the author's approach to bridge the gap between those who believe in climate change and those who don't?

CHAPTER 4

WHAT BUSINESS LEADERS SAY

Business leaders, like decision makers in other walks of life, have formed opinions about climate change based on the information available to them. These opinions are strategically very important, since global warming will impact their particular companies to varying degrees depending on the nature of the individual business. A business leader needs to be well informed in order to make smart decisions when making short- and long-term plans for his or her company's future.

Problems arise when the leader of a company with vested interests in the oil business, for example, promotes the view that climate change is not happening (or if it does exist it is not caused by human activity). What this individual says may not reflect what he or she truly believes. In the case of Exxon, for example, the company's own scientists conducted research on climate change decades ago. They learned that global warming was indeed occurring and that their company was partly responsible for it. Yet Exxon claimed that global warming didn't exist.

This chapter starts with an article about Bill Gates' beliefs on climate change—and how he believes the government must provide scientists with incentives that encourage them to change our world for the better.

"BILL GATES: THE WORLD NEEDS 'A MIRACLE' TO SOLVE MAN-MADE GLOBAL WARMING," BY CHRIS WHITE, FROM THE *DAILY CALLER*, FEBRUARY 23, 2016

THE DAILY CALLER NEWS FOUNDATION

Bill Gates wrote in a letter posted on his website the world will "need a miracle" to come up with a solution to man-made global warming.

Gates argued things look bleak right now for the Earth's climate, as carbon emissions are unlikely to be dialed down anytime soon, unless of course younger generations can find a magic button to whisk away the warming.

In his annual letter, which was primarily addressed to younger millennials, Gates notes he sees the climate problem through a basic math formula: P x S x E x C =

carbon dioxide. The P represents population, S represents the number of services each person uses, E means energy and C is carbon dioxide created by energy.

The world can only be saved, according to Gates, when carbon dioxide production, or C, goes down to zero.

"When I say 'miracle,' I don't mean something that's impossible. I've seen miracles happen before. The personal computer. The Internet. The polio vaccine. None of them happened by chance. They are the result of research and development and the human capacity to innovate," Gates said during an interview with Bloomberg Business.

He added: "In this case, however, time is not on our side. Every day we are releasing more and more CO_2 into our atmosphere and making our climate change problem even worse. We need a massive amount of research into thousands of new ideas—even ones that might sound a little crazy—if we want to get to zero emissions by the end of this century."

Gates said that he chose to direct his report at young people because he believes they are the best option going forward.

"With scientific innovation, you see that people in their 20s get a depth of knowledge and a willingness to look at things in a different way," Gates said about millennials. "So, I would say it's likely that if an energy miracle comes in the next 15 years, key participants will be the teenagers of today."

A prescription for global warming requires a mixture of "risk takers" and "dark horses." In short, the world needs people willing to conjure up innovative ideas that seemingly come out of nowhere.

Gates went on to note during the interview that the modern internal combustion engine was one clear example of a dark horse.

"Then, there was this dark horse where they were exploding things in these metal boxes called internal combustion. They kept blowing things up, but because of the energy density of gasoline, the private market weighed the relative merits, and two out of three approaches are footnotes in history," Gates said.

The billionaire also suggested young people will need role models if they are to become world leaders in the alternative energy market. And of course, Gates offered a bevy of people he thinks are great role models for millennials.

"I think Steve Jobs, Mark Zuckerberg, Larry Page— some of the IT people that took a risk and did amazing work that has changed the world," he told Bloomberg Business.

He included in his list of role models Techno-wonder Elon Musk, telling the interviewer that Musk "would be great" for young people to tether themselves to in the future.

Gates noted in a November 2015 Atlantic interview that a carbon tax is the best way to get innovators to solve climate change – in essence, young innovators will need role models and the giant hand of the government if they are to bring about the miracle Gates thinks is possible.

"Even if you have a new energy source that costs the same as today's and emits no CO_2, it will be uncertain compared with what's tried-and-true and already oper- ating at unbelievable scale and has gotten through all the regulatory problems," Gates told The Atlantic.

The Microsoft creator turned philanthropist concluded by arguing people grow more disgusted by global warming and pollution the wealthier they become.

Wealth "is the leading indicator of things that we will change. We will change our energy economy" and our climate because we will become unhappy about it.

Content created by The Daily Caller News Foundation is available without charge to any eligible news publisher that can provide a large audience. For licensing opportunities of our original content, please contact licensing@dailycall-ernewsfoundation.org.

1. According to Bill Gates, why does he think young people have the best chance of solving climate change? Do you agree or disagree?

"AS NY STATE PROBES EXXON, OIL GIANT TARGETS THE JOURNALISTS WHO EXPOSED CLIMATE CHANGE COVER-UP," FROM *DEMOCRACY NOW!*, DECEMBER 2, 2015

Oil giant ExxonMobil is under criminal investigation in New York over claims it lied to the public and investors about the risks of climate change. Now Exxon is fighting back against the journalists who exposed how it concealed its own findings dating back to the 1970s that fossil fuels cause global warming, alter the climate and melt the Arctic ice. Students at Columbia Journalism School collaborated with the Los Angeles Times on two of the exposés. Exxon accused the students of producing inaccurate and misleading articles. In its complaint, Exxon also referred to the "numerous and productive relationships" ExxonMobil has with Columbia—Exxon has donated nearly $220,000 to the school. On Tuesday, Steve Coll, the dean of the Columbia Journalism School, responded to Exxon's critiques after an extensive review. Our guest Bill McKibben has been following the Exxon exposés closely. In October he was arrested after staging a one-man protest at a local Exxon station. He held a sign reading, "This pump temporarily closed because ExxonMobil lied about climate."

AMY GOODMAN: We turn right now to the oil giant ExxonMobil. It's under criminal investigation in New York over claims it lied to the public and investors about the risks of climate change. Now Exxon is fighting back against the journalists who exposed how Exxon concealed its own findings dating back to the 1970s that fossil fuels cause global warming, alter the climate and melt the Arctic ice. Students at Columbia Journalism School collaborated with the *Los Angeles Times* on two of the exposés. Exxon accused the students of producing inaccurate and misleading articles. In its complaint, Exxon also referred to the, quote, «numerous and productive relationships» ExxonMobil has with Columbia—Exxon has donated nearly $220,000 to the school.

On Tuesday, Steve Coll, the dean of the Columbia Journalism School, responded to Exxon's critique, written to Columbia's president, after an extensive review. Coll wrote, quote, "Your letter disputes the substance of the two articles in a number of respects, but consists largely of attacks on the project's journalists. I have concluded that your allegations are unsupported by evidence. More than that, I have been troubled to discover that you have made serious allegations of professional misconduct in your letter against members of the project [team] even though you or your Media Relations colleagues possess email records showing that your allegations are false," Coll wrote.

Well, our guest, Bill McKibben, co-founder of 350.org, has been following the Exxon exposés closely. In October, he was arrested after staging a one-man protest at his local Exxon station in Vermont. He held a sign reading, "This pump temporarily closed because Exxon-Mobil lied about climate."

Bill McKibben, you're a journalist yourself. Talk about the significance of ExxonMobil writing this letter of complaint to the president of Columbia University, Lee Bollinger, who then turned the letter over to Steve Coll, also a leading journalist, who did an investigation of Columbia Journalism School students.

BILL McKIBBEN: So, Exxon is never very subtle, and this was a particularly heavy-handed instance of it. Their letter to Columbia can only be described as thuggish. It carried every kind of implication about how they would do one thing or another to them if they didn't get satisfaction. But I think they might think twice before they do it again. The letter that came back from Steve Coll at Columbia was a six-page masterpiece of dissection. It sort of shows what happens when real reporters go up against PR people. It was remarkable, Amy.

These stories—I mean, this is just Exxon trying to kick up smoke around the edges. There's no problem with the stories. They're incredibly powerful, incredibly true, and so salient to where we sit today. If Exxon had told the truth about what it knew 25 years ago, we would not be needing to have COP21. We would have, sometime around COP3 or 4, really gotten down to work as a planet. And this problem wouldn't be solved yet, but we wouldn't have wasted 25 years in phony debate.

AMY GOODMAN: And we did an extensive look at this on *Democracy Now!* on the investigation of both InsideClimate News, the Pulitzer Prize-winning journalistic organization, and *Los Angeles Times*, which, of course, has also won many Pulitzers. But the evidence that—they had top scientists. They were deeply concerned about this, doing very good work, and saw climate change as real. But then what happened?

BILL McKIBBEN: Well, then they—instead of acting on their knowledge, they instead set up the architecture of denial and disinformation. There was a remarkable piece that came out, a study that came out in *Nature* yesterday, documenting the fact that the money from Exxon and the Koch brothers constituted the sort of epicenter of denial. This was one of these big data analyses that traced the links between thousands of different organizations and newsletters and front groups, and they traced it back to Exxon. That's why the secretary of state yesterday, John Kerry, in a pretty rare moment, in *Rolling Stone* really let loose on Exxon and said that it was—if these allegations were true, it was worse than the tobacco industry and a betrayal of everything that it meant to be a responsible corporation.

AMY GOODMAN: And the significance of the New York state attorney general, Eric Schneiderman, launching a criminal probe into ExxonMobil?

BILL McKIBBEN: Well, you can be sure that Exxon is taking it seriously because yesterday they hired one of the most expensive lawyers in the country, Theodore Wells, most recently famous for having written the Deflategate report about the New England Patriots in last year's football season. Theodore Wells, from Paul, Weiss, Rifkind in New York, is now Exxon's—on retainer for Exxon to try and battle these allegations. But good luck to him, because the evidence, down there in black and white, is pretty stunning. Remember, at the best, no one is saying—I mean, the best that anyone is saying is that Exxon was merely morally reprehensible, not outright criminal. That's the best defense that anybody has mounted for them so far.

AMY GOODMAN: So, we're not talking about a civil probe, we're talking about a criminal probe. This could land Exxon officials in jail?

BILL McKIBBEN: Well, who knows? I mean, they haven't said—at the moment, they're just subpoenaing documents. We're still at the beginning stages of this. And, of course, the great hope is that other attorney generals—Kamala Harris in California, for instance—will, we hope, join in at some point, and that the Department of

Justice—360,000 Americans have petitioned the Department of Justice, asking them to investigate Exxon.

AMY GOODMAN: And on the issue of ExxonMobil writing the letter to the president of Columbia University, in it mentioning the amount of money they have given to Columbia, do you see this as an attack on freedom of the press?

BILL McKIBBEN: Oh, I mean, who knows what precisely they had in mind? But Exxon has attacked the freedom of thought of an entire planet for 25 years. They knew the truth, and they hid it. They told people things that they knew not to be true. There is no more devastating attack on the freedom of thought than that.

1. Would you consider Exxon's actions described in this article as an "attack on the freedom of the press"? Why or why not?

"MORE THAN EXXON: BIG OIL COMPANIES FOR YEARS SHARED DAMNING CLIMATE RESEARCH," BY LAUREN MCCAULEY, FROM COMMON DREAMS, DECEMBER 22, 2015

NEW INVESTIGATIVE REPORTING EXPOSES A TASK FORCE HEADED BY THE AMERICAN PETROLEUM INSTITUTE ALSO KNEW ABOUT GLOBAL WARMING SINCE THE 1970'S

It wasn't just Exxon that knew fossil fuels were cooking the planet.

New investigative reporting by Neela Banerjee with *Inside Climate News* revealed on Tuesday that scientists and engineers from nearly every major U.S. and multinational oil and gas company may have for decades known about the impacts of carbon emissions on the climate.

Between 1979 and 1983, the American Petroleum Institute (API), the industry's most powerful lobby group, ran a task force for fossil fuel companies to "monitor and share climate research," according to internal documents obtained by *Inside Climate News*.

According to the reporting:

Like Exxon, the companies also expressed a willingness to understand the links between their product, greater CO_2 concentrations and the climate, the papers reveal. Some corporations ran their own research units as well, although they were smaller and less ambitious than Exxon's and focused on climate modeling, said James J. Nelson, the former director of the task force.

"It was a fact-finding task force," Nelson said in an interview. "We wanted to look at emerging science, the implications of it and where improvements could be made, if possible, to reduce emissions."

The 'CO$_2$ and Climate Task Force,' which changed in 1980 its name to the 'Climate and Energy Task Force,' included researchers from Exxon, Mobil, Chevron, Amoco, Phillips, Texaco, Shell, Sunoco, and Sohio, among others.

One memo by an Exxon task force representative pointed to 1979 "background paper on CO$_2$," which "predicted when the first clear effects of climate change might be felt," noting that the concentration of carbon dioxide in the atmosphere was rising steadily.

And at a February 1980 meeting in New York, the task force invited Professor John A. Laurmann of Stanford University to brief members about climate science.

"In his conclusions section, Laurmann estimated that the amount of CO$_2$ in the atmosphere would double in 2038, which he said would likely lead to a 2.5 degrees Celsius rise in global average temperatures with ‹major economic consequences,›» Banerjee reports. He then told the task force that models showed a 5 degrees Celsius rise by 2067, with ‹globally catastrophic effects,›» Banerjee reports.

The documents show that API members, at one point, considered an alternative path in the face of these dire predictions:

Bruce S. Bailey of Texaco offered "for consideration" the idea that "an overall goal of the Task Force should be to help develop ground rules for energy release of fuels and the cleanup of fuels as they relate to CO_2 creation," according to the minutes of a meeting on Feb. 29, 1980.

The minutes also show that the task force discussed a "potential area" for research and development that called for it to "'Investigate the Market Penetration Requirements of Introducing a New Energy Source into World Wide Use.' This would include the technical implications of energy source changeover, research timing and requirements."

"Yet," Banerjee notes, "by the 1990s, it was clear that API had opted for a markedly different approach to the threat of climate change."

The lobby group teamed up with Exxon and others to form the Global Climate Coalition (GCC), which successfully lobbied the U.S. to withdraw from the Kyoto Protocol.

The damning revelations are the latest in an ongoing investigation into what the fossil fuel industry knew about climate change and then suppressed for decades — all while continuing to profit from the planet's destruction.

Reports that Exxon, specifically, lied about climate change were published early October in the Los Angeles Times, mirroring a separate but similar investigation byInside Climate News in September. Those findings set off a storm of outrage, including a probe by the New York Attorney General.

Nelson, a former head of the API task force, told Banerjee that with the growing powers of the Environmental Protection Agency (EPA) in the early 1980's, API decided to shift gears.

"They took the environmental unit and put it into the political department, which was primarily lobbyists," he said. "They weren't focused on doing research or on improving the oil industry's impact on pollution. They were less interested in pushing the envelope of science and more interested in how to make it more advantageous politically or economically for the oil industry. That's not meant as a criticism. It's just a fact of life."

1. Why do you think that by the 1990s the major oil companies, with full knowledge of their dangerous contribution to climate change, abandoned any consideration of changing over to less harmful sources of energy?

CHAPTER 5

SPIRITUAL AND MORAL PERSPECTIVES

M any spiritual leaders of the world's major religions, including Pope Francis of the Catholic Church, have spoken out about the dangers that climate change poses for all of humanity. They point out that the climate crisis has been caused by human activity and that we have the moral responsibility to do all we can to stop global warming before it destroys us. It is somewhat rare for the leaders of major religions to agree so fully on such a political issue.

Journalist Christopher Booker, however, looks at the "religious" aspect of global warming from a different standpoint. He argues that environmentalists and climate activists have turned their "quasi-religious faith" in scientists' computer models into dogma, where science takes precedence above all else and criticism is not tolerated.

EXCERPT FROM "ENCYCLICAL LETTER *LAUDATO SI'* OF THE HOLY FATHER FRANCIS ON CARE FOR OUR COMMON HOME," FROM THE HOLY SEE, MAY 24, 2015

CLIMATE AS A COMMON GOOD

23. The climate is a common good, belonging to all and meant for all. At the global level, it is a complex system linked to many of the essential conditions for human life. A very solid scientific consensus indicates that we are presently witnessing a disturbing warming of the climatic system. In recent decades this warming has been accompanied by a constant rise in the sea level and, it would appear, by an increase of extreme weather events, even if a scientifically determinable cause cannot be assigned to each particular phenomenon. Humanity is called to recognize the need for changes of lifestyle, production and consumption, in order to combat this warming or at least the human causes which produce or aggravate it. It is true that there are other factors (such as volcanic activity, variations in the earth's orbit and axis, the solar cycle), yet a number of scientific studies indicate that most global warming in recent decades is due to the great concentration of greenhouse gases (carbon dioxide, methane, nitrogen oxides and others) released mainly as a result of human activity. As these gases build up in the atmosphere, they hamper the escape of heat produced by sunlight at the earth's surface. The problem is aggravated by a model of development based on the intensive use of fossil fuels, which is at the heart of the worldwide energy

system. Another determining factor has been an increase in changed uses of the soil, principally deforestation for agricultural purposes.

24. Warming has effects on the carbon cycle. It creates a vicious circle which aggravates the situation even more, affecting the availability of essential resources like drinking water, energy and agricultural production in warmer regions, and leading to the extinction of part of the planet's biodiversity. The melting in the polar ice caps and in high altitude plains can lead to the dangerous release of methane gas, while the decomposition of frozen organic material can further increase the emission of carbon dioxide. Things are made worse by the loss of tropical forests which would otherwise help to mitigate climate change. Carbon dioxide pollution increases the acidification of the oceans and compromises the marine food chain. If present trends continue, this century may well witness extraordinary climate change and an unprecedented destruction of ecosystems, with serious consequences for all of us. A rise in the sea level, for example, can create extremely serious situations, if we consider that a quarter of the world's population lives on the coast or nearby, and that the majority of our megacities are situated in coastal areas.

25. Climate change is a global problem with grave implications: environmental, social, economic, political and for the distribution of goods. It represents one of the principal challenges facing humanity in our day. Its worst impact will probably be felt by developing countries in coming decades. Many of the poor live in areas particularly affected by phenomena related to warming, and their means of subsistence are largely dependent on

natural reserves and ecosystemic services such as agriculture, fishing and forestry. They have no other financial activities or resources which can enable them to adapt to climate change or to face natural disasters, and their access to social services and protection is very limited. For example, changes in climate, to which animals and plants cannot adapt, lead them to migrate; this in turn affects the livelihood of the poor, who are then forced to leave their homes, with great uncertainty for their future and that of their children. There has been a tragic rise in the number of migrants seeking to flee from the growing poverty caused by environmental degradation. They are not recognized by international conventions as refugees; they bear the loss of the lives they have left behind, without enjoying any legal protection whatsoever. Sadly, there is widespread indifference to such suffering, which is even now taking place throughout our world. Our lack of response to these tragedies involving our brothers and sisters points to the loss of that sense of responsibility for our fellow men and women upon which all civil society is founded.

26. Many of those who possess more resources and economic or political power seem mostly to be concerned with masking the problems or concealing their symptoms, simply making efforts to reduce some of the negative impacts of climate change. However, many of these symptoms indicate that such effects will continue to worsen if we continue with current models of production and consumption. There is an urgent need to develop policies so that, in the next few years, the emission of carbon dioxide and other highly polluting gases can be drastically reduced, for example, substituting for fossil fuels

and developing sources of renewable energy. Worldwide there is minimal access to clean and renewable energy. There is still a need to develop adequate storage technologies. Some countries have made considerable progress, although it is far from constituting a significant proportion. Investments have also been made in means of production and transportation which consume less energy and require fewer raw materials, as well as in methods of construction and renovating buildings which improve their energy efficiency. But these good practices are still far from widespread.

1. Why does Pope Francis say that the climate is a common good?

2. According to Francis, why will the worst impact of climate change be felt by the people in developing countries?

"ISLAMIC DECLARATION ON GLOBAL CLIMATE CHANGE," FROM THE INTERNATIONAL ISLAMIC CLIMATE CHANGE SYMPOSIUM, 2015

IN THE NAME OF ALLAH, MOST MERCIFUL, MOST COMPASSIONATE

PREAMBLE

- God – Whom we know as Allah – has created the universe in all its diversity, richness and vitality: the stars, the sun and moon, the earth and all its communities of living beings. All these reflect and manifest the boundless glory and mercy of their Creator. All created beings by nature serve and glorify their Maker, all bow to their Lord's will. We human beings are created to serve the Lord of all beings, to work the greatest good we can for all the species, individuals, and generations of God's creatures.

- Our planet has existed for billions of years and climate change in itself is not new. The earth's climate has gone through phases wet and dry, cold and warm, in response to many natural factors. Most of these changes have been gradual, so that the forms and communities of life have adjusted accordingly. There have been catastrophic climate changes that brought about mass extinctions, but over time, life adjusted even to these impacts, flowering anew in the emergence of balanced ecosystems such as those we treasure today. Climate change in the past was also instrumental in laying down immense stores of fossil fuels from which we derive benefits today. Ironically, our unwise and short-sighted use of these resources is now resulting in the destruction of the very conditions that have made our life on earth possible.

- The pace of Global climate change today is of a different order of magnitude from the gradual changes that previously occurred throughout the most recent era, the Cenozoic. Moreover, it is human-induced: we have now become a force dominating nature. The epoch in which we live has increasingly been described in geological terms as the Anthropocene, or "Age of Humans". Our species, though selected to be a caretaker or steward (khalifah) on the earth, has been the cause of such corruption and devastation on it that we are in danger ending life as we know it on our planet. This current rate of climate change cannot be sustained, and the earth's fine equilibrium (mīzān) may soon be lost. As we humans are woven into the fabric of the natural world, its gifts are for us to savour. But the same fossil fuels that helped us achieve most of the prosperity we see today are the main cause of climate change. Excessive pollution from fossil fuels threatens to destroy the gifts bestowed on us by God, whom we know as Allah – gifts such as a functioning climate, healthy air to breathe, regular seasons, and living oceans. But our attitude to these gifts has been short-sighted, and we have abused them. What will future generations say of us, who leave them a degraded planet as our legacy? How will we face our Lord and Creator?
- We note that the Millennium Ecosystem Assessment (UNEP, 2005) and backed by over 1300 scientists from

95 countries, found that "overall, people have made greater changes to ecosystems in the last half of the 20th century than at any time in human history... these changes have enhanced human well-being, but have been accompanied by ever increasing degradation (of our environment)."

"Human activity is putting such a strain on the natural functions of the earth that the ability of the planet's ecosystems to sustain future generations can no longer be taken for granted."

- Nearly ten years later, and in spite of the numerous conferences that have taken place to try to agree on a successor to the Kyoto Protocol, the overall state of the Earth has steadily deteriorated. A study by the Intergovernmental Panel on Climate Change (IPCC) comprising representatives from over 100 nations published in March 2014 gave five reasons for concern. In summary, they are:
- Ecosystems and human cultures are already at risk from climate change;
- Risks resulting from climate change caused by extreme events such as heat waves, extreme precipitation and coastal flooding are on the rise;
- These risks are unevenly distributed, and are generally greater for the poor and disadvantaged communities of every country, at all levels of development;
- Foreseeable impacts will affect adversely Earth's biodiversity, the goods and services provided by our ecosystems, and our overall global economy;
- The Earth's core physical systems themselves are at risk of abrupt and irreversible changes.

We are driven to conclude from these warnings that there are serious flaws in the way we have used natural resources — the sources of life on Earth. An urgent and radical reappraisal is called for. Humankind cannot afford the slow progress we have seen in all the COP (Conference of Parties — climate change negotiations) processes since the Millennium Ecosystem Assessment was published in 2005, or the present deadlock.

- In the brief period since the Industrial Revolution, humans have consumed much of the non-renewable resources which have taken the earth 250 million years to produce – all in the name of economic development and human progress. We note with alarm the combined impacts of rising per capita consumption combined with the rising human population. We also note with alarm the multi-national scramble now taking place for more fossil fuel deposits under the dissolving ice caps in the arctic regions. We are accelerating our own destruction through these processes.
- Leading climate scientists now believe that a rise of two degrees centigrade in global temperature, which is considered to be the "tipping point", is now very unlikely to be avoided if we continue with business-as-usual; other leading climate scientists consider 1.5 degrees centigrade to be a more likely "tipping point". This is the point considered to be the threshold for catastrophic climate change, which will expose yet more millions of people and countless other creatures to drought, hunger and flooding. The brunt of this will continue to be borne by the poor, as the Earth experiences a drastic increase in levels of carbon in the atmosphere brought on in the period since the onset of the industrial revolution.

1.8 It is alarming that in spite of all the warnings and predictions, the successor to the Kyoto Protocol which should have been in place by 2012, has been delayed. It is essential that all countries, especially the more developed nations, increase their efforts and adopt the pro-active approach needed to halt and hopefully eventually reverse the damage being wrought.

WE AFFIRM

- We affirm that Allah is the Lord and Sustainer (Rabb) of all beings

ﻥَﻟْﺤَﻤْﺪُ ﻟِﻠَّﻪِ ﺭَﺑِّ ﺍﻟْﻌَﺎﻟَﻤِﻴﻦَ

Praise be to Allah, Lord and Sustainer of all beings

Qur'an 1: 1

He is the One Creator – He is al-Khāliq

ﻭَﻩُ ﺍﻟﻠَّﻪُ ﺍﻟْﺨَﺎﻟِﻖُ ﺍﻟْﺒَﺎﺭِﺉُ ﺍﻟْﻤُﺼَﻮِّﺭُ

He is Allah – the Creator, the Maker, the Giver of Form

Qur'an 59: 24

ﺍﻟَّﺬِﻱ ﺃَﺣْﺴَﻦَ ﻛُﻞَّ ﺷَﻲْﺀٍ ﺧَﻠَﻘَﻪُ

He Who has perfected every thing He has created

Qur'an 32: 7

Nothing that He creates is without value: each thing is created bi 'l-haqq, in truth and for right.

وَمَا خَلَقْنَا السَّمَاوَاتِ وَالْأَرْضَ وَمَا بَيْنَهُمَا لَاعِبِينَ مَا خَلَقْنَاهُمَا إِلَّا بِالْحَقِّ

And We did not create the heavens and earth and that between them in play. We have not created them but in truth

Qur'an 44: 38

- We affirm that He encompasses all of His creation – He is al-Muhīt

وَلِلَّهِ مَا فِي السَّمَاوَاتِ وَمَا فِي الْأَرْضِ وَكَانَ اللَّهُ بِكُلِّ شَيْءٍ مُحِيطًا

All that is in the heavens and the earth belongs to Allah.

Allah encompasses all things

Qur'an 4: 125

- We affirm that –

God created the Earth in perfect equilibrium (mīzān);

By His immense mercy we have been given fertile land, fresh air, clean water and all the good things on Earth that makes our lives here viable and delightful;

The Earth functions in natural seasonal rhythms and cycles: a climate in which living beings – including humans – thrive;

The present climate change catastrophe is a result of the human disruption of this balance –

وَالسَّمَاءَ رَفَعَهَا وَوَضَعَ الْمِيزَانَ

أَلَّا تَطْغَوْا فِي الْمِيزَانِ

وَأَقِيمُوا الْوَزْنَ بِالْقِسْطِ وَلَا تُخْسِرُوا الْمِيزَانَ

وَالْأَرْضَ وَضَعَهَا لِلْأَنَامِ

He raised the heaven and established the balance

So that you would not transgress the balance.

Give just weight – do not skimp in the balance.

He laid out the earth for all living creatures.

Qur'an 55: 7-10

We affirm the natural state (fitrah) of God's creation –

فَأَقِمْ وَجْهَكَ لِلدِّينِ حَنِيفًا فِطْرَةَ اللَّهِ الَّتِي فَطَرَ النَّاسَ عَلَيْهَا

لَا تَبْدِيلَ لِخَلْقِ اللَّهِ ذَلِكَ الدِّينُ الْقَيِّمُ وَلَكِنَّ أَكْثَرَ النَّاسِ لَا يَعْلَمُونَ

So set your face firmly towards the (natural) Way

As a pure, natural believer

Allah's natural pattern on which He made mankind

There is no changing Allah's creation.

That is the true (natural) Way

But most people do not know it.

Quran 30: 30

2.5 We recognize the corruption (fasād) that humans have caused on the Earth due to our relentless pursuit of economic growth and consumption. Its consequences have been –

- Global climate change, which is our present concern, in addition to:
- Contamination and befoulment of the atmosphere, land, inland water systems, and seas;
- Soil erosion, deforestation and desertification;
- Damage to human health, including a host of modern-day diseases.

ظَهَرَ الْفَسَادُ فِي الْبَرِّ وَالْبَحْرِ بِمَا كَسَبَتْ أَيْدِي النَّاسِ لِيُذِيقَهُمْ بَعْضَ الَّذِي عَمِلُوا لَعَلَّهُمْ يَرْجِعُونَ

Corruption has appeared on land and sea

Because of what people's own hands have wrought,

So that they may taste something of what they have done;

So that hopefully they will turn back.

Qur'an 30: 41

- We recognize that we are but a minuscule part of the divine order, yet within that order, we are exceptionally powerful beings, and have the responsibility to establish good and avert evil in every way we can. We also recognize that –
- We are but one of the multitude of living beings with whom we share the Earth;
- We have no right to oppress the rest of creation or cause it harm;

135

- Intelligence and conscience behoove us, as our faith commands, to treat all things with care and awe (taqwa) of their Creator, compassion (rahmah) and utmost good (ihsan).

وَمَا مِن دَآبَّةٍ فِي الأَرْضِ وَلَا طَائِرٍ يَطِيرُ بِجَنَاحَيْهِ إِلَّا أُمَمٌ أَمْثَالُكُم

There is no animal on the earth, or any bird that wings its flight, but is a community like you.

Qur'an 6: 38

لَخَلْقُ السَّمَاوَاتِ وَالأَرْضِ أَكْبَرُ مِنْ خَلْقِ النَّاسِ وَلَكِنَّ أَكْثَرَ النَّاسِ لَا يَعْلَمُونَ

The creation of the heavens and the earth

Is far greater than the creation of mankind,

But most of mankind do not know it

Qur'an 40: 57

- We recognize that we are accountable for all our actions –

فَمَن يَعْمَلْ مِثْقَالَ ذَرَّةٍ خَيْرًا يَرَهُ

وَمَن يَعْمَلْ مِثْقَالَ ذَرَّةٍ شَرًّا يَرَهُ

Then he who has done an atom's weight of good, shall see it;

and he who has done an atom's weight of evil, shall see it.

Qur'an 99:6-8

2.8 In view of these considerations we affirm that our responsibility as Muslims is to act according to the example of the Prophet Muhammad (God's peace and blessings be upon him) who –

- Declared and protected the rights of all living beings, outlawed the custom of burying infant girls alive, prohibited killing living beings for sport, guided his companions to conserve water even in washing for prayer, forbade the felling of trees in the desert, ordered a man who had taken some nestlings from their nest to return them to their mother, and when he came upon a man who had lit a fire on an anthill, commanded, "Put it out, put it out!";
- Established inviolable zones (harams) around Makkah and Al-Madinah, within which native plants may not be felled or cut and wild animals may not be hunted or disturbed;
- Established protected areas (himas) for the conservation and sustainable use of rangelands, plant cover and wildlife.
- Lived a frugal life, free of excess, waste, and ostentation;
- Renewed and recycled his meagre possessions by repairing or giving them away;
- Ate simple, healthy food, which only occasionally included meat;
- Took delight in the created world; and
- Was, in the words of the Qur'an, "a mercy to all beings."

WE CALL

3.1 We call upon the Conference of the Parties (COP) to the United Nations Framework Convention on Climate

Change (UNFCCC) and the Meeting of the Parties (MOP) to the Kyoto Protocol taking place in Paris this December, 2015 to bring their discussions to an equitable and binding conclusion, bearing in mind –

- The scientific consensus on climate change, which is to stabilize greenhouse gas concentration in the atmosphere at a level that would prevent dangerous anthropogenic interference with the climate systems;
- The need to set clear targets and monitoring systems;
- The dire consequences to planet earth if we do not do so;
- The enormous responsibility the COP shoulders on behalf of the rest of humanity, including leading the rest of us to a new way of relating to God's Earth.

3.2 We particularly call on the well-off nations and oil-producing states to –

- Lead the way in phasing out their greenhouse gas emissions as early as possible and no later than the middle of the century;
- Provide generous financial and technical support to the less well-off to achieve a phase-out of green-house gases as early as possible;
- Recognize the moral obligation to reduce consumption so that the poor may benefit from what is left of the earth's non-renewable resources;
- Stay within the '2 degree' limit, or, preferably, within the '1.5 degree' limit, bearing in mind that two-thirds of the earth's proven fossil fuel reserves remain in the ground;
- Re-focus their concerns from unethical profit from the environment, to that of preserving it and elevating the condition of the world's poor.

- Invest in the creation of a green economy.

3.3 We call on the people of all nations and their leaders to –
- Aim to phase out greenhouse gas emissions as soon as possible in order to stabilize greenhouse gas concentrations in the atmosphere;
- Commit themselves to 100 % renewable energy and/ or a zero emissions strategy as early as possible, to mitigate the environmental impact of their activities;
- Invest in decentralized renewable energy, which is the best way to reduce poverty and achieve sustainable development;
- Realize that to chase after unlimited economic growth in a planet that is finite and already overloaded is not viable. Growth must be pursued wisely and in moderation; placing a priority on increasing the resilience of all, and especially the most vulnerable, to the climate change impacts already underway and expected to continue for many years to come.
- Set in motion a fresh model of wellbeing, based on an alternative to the current financial model which depletes resources, degrades the environment, and deepens inequality.
- Prioritise adaptation efforts with appropriate support to the vulnerable countries with the least capacity to adapt. And to vulnerable groups, including indigenous peoples, women and children.

3.4 We call upon corporations, finance, and the business sector to –
- Shoulder the consequences of their profit-making activities, and take a visibly more active role in

reducing their carbon footprint and other forms of impact upon the natural environment;

- In order to mitigate the environmental impact of their activities, commit themselves to 100 % renewable energy and/or a zero emissions strategy as early as possible and shift investments into renewable energy;
- Change from the current business model which is based on an unsustainable escalating economy, and to adopt a circular economy that is wholly sustainable;
- Pay more heed to social and ecological responsibilities, particularly to the extent that they extract and utilize scarce resources;
- Assist in the divestment from the fossil fuel driven economy and the scaling up of renewable energy and other ecological alternatives.

3.5 We call on all groups to join us in collaboration, co-operation and friendly competition in this endeavour and we welcome the significant contributions taken by other faiths, as we can all be winners in this race

وَلِكُلٍّ نِكِلَن مَكُوۡبُلُقۡو افَسۡتَبِقُوا الۡخَيۡرَاتِ مَاۤ في يِ مَ فَاتَاكُم فَاسۡتَبِقُوا الۡخَيۡرَاتِ

He (God) wanted to test you regarding what has

come to you. So compete with each other

in doing good deeds.

Qur'an 5: 48

If we each offer the best of our respective traditions, we may yet see a way through our difficulties.

3.6 Finally, we call on all Muslims wherever they may be –

Heads of state
Political leaders
Business community
UNFCCC delegates
Religious leaders and scholars
Mosque congregations
Islamic endowments (awqaf)
Educators and educational institutions
Community leaders
Civil society activists
Non-governmental organisations
Communications and media

وَلَن تَمْشِ في الأَرْضِ مَرَحًا إِنَّكَ لَن تَخْرِقَ الأَرْضَ وَلَن تَبْلُغَ الْجِبَالَ طُولاً

Do not strut arrogantly on the earth.

You will never split the earth apart

nor will you ever rival the mountains' stature.

Qur'an 17: 37

We bear in mind the words of our Prophet (peace and blessings be upon him):

The world is sweet and verdant, and verily Allah has made you stewards in it, and He sees how you acquit yourselves
Hadīth related by Muslim from Abu Saʿīd Al-Khudrī

141

1. How is today's climate change different from previous changes in the world's climate?

2. The great changes people have made to ecosystems in the last half of the twentieth century have enhanced human well being. But these changes have caused increasing degradation of the environment. Do you think these changes have been worth it? Why or why not?

EXCERPT FROM "THE TIME TO ACT IS NOW: A BUDDHIST DECLARATION ON CLIMATE CHANGE," MAY 14, 2015

Today we live in a time of great crisis, confronted by the gravest challenge that humanity has ever faced: the ecological consequences of our own collective karma. The scientific consensus is overwhelming: human activity is triggering environmental breakdown on a planetary scale. Global warming, in particular, is happening much faster than previously predicted, most obviously at the North Pole. For hundreds of thousands of years, the Arctic Ocean has been covered by an area of sea-ice as large as Australia—but now this is melting rapidly. In 2007 the

Intergovernmental Panel on Climate Change (IPCC) forecast that the Arctic might be free of summer sea ice by 2100. It is now apparent that this could occur within a decade or two. Greenland's vast ice-sheet is also melting more quickly than expected. The rise in sea-level this century will be at least one meter—enough to flood many coastal cities and vital rice-growing areas such as the Mekong Delta in Vietnam.

Glaciers all over the world are receding quickly. If current economic policies continue, the glaciers of the Tibetan Plateau, source of the great rivers that provide water for billions of people in Asia, are likely to disappear by mid-century. Severe drought and crop failures are already affecting Australia and Northern China. Major reports—from the IPCC, United Nations, European Union, and International Union for Conservation of Nature—agree that, without a collective change of direction, dwindling supplies of water, food and other resources could create famine conditions, resource battles, and mass migration by mid-century—perhaps by 2030, according to the U.K.'s chief scientific advisor.

Global warming plays a major role in other ecological crises, including the loss of many plant and animal species that share this Earth with us. Oceanographers report that half the carbon released by burning fossil fuels has been absorbed by the oceans, increasing their acidity by about 30%. Acidification is disrupting calcification of shells and coral reefs, as well as threatening plankton growth, the source of the food chain for most life in the sea.

Eminent biologists and U.N. reports concur that "business-as-usual" will drive half of all species on Earth to extinction within this century. Collectively, we are violating the first precept—"do not harm living beings"— on the largest possible scale. And we cannot foresee the biological consequences for human life when so many species that invisibly contribute to our own well-being vanish from the planet.

Many scientists have concluded that the survival of human civilization is at stake. We have reached a critical juncture in our biological and social evolution. There has never been a more important time in history to bring the resources of Buddhism to bear on behalf of all living beings. The four noble truths provide a framework for diagnosing our current situation and formulating appropriate guidelines— because the threats and disasters we face ultimately stem from the human mind, and therefore require profound changes within our minds. If personal suffering stems from craving and ignorance—from the three poisons of greed, ill will, and delusion—the same applies to the suffering that afflicts us on a collective scale. Our ecological emergency is a larger version of the perennial human predicament. Both as individuals and as a species, we suffer from a sense of self that feels disconnected not only from other people but from the Earth itself. As Thich Nhat Hanh has said, "We are here to awaken from the illusion of our separateness." We need to wake up and realize that the Earth is our mother as well as our home— and in this case the umbilical cord binding us to her cannot be severed. When the Earth becomes sick, we become sick, because we are part of her.

Our present economic and technological relationships with the rest of the biosphere are unsustainable. To survive the rough transitions ahead, our lifestyles and expectations must change. This involves new habits as well as new values. The Buddhist teaching that the overall health of the individual and society depends upon inner well-being, and not merely upon economic indicators, helps us determine the personal and social changes we must make.

Individually, we must adopt behaviors that increase everyday ecological awareness and reduce our "carbon footprint". Those of us in the advanced economies need to retrofit and insulate our homes and workplaces for energy efficiency; lower thermostats in winter and raise them in summer; use high efficiency light bulbs and appliances; turn off unused electrical appliances; drive the most fuel-efficient cars possible, and reduce meat consumption in favor of a healthy, environmentally-friendly plant-based diet.

These personal activities will not by themselves be sufficient to avert future calamity. We must also make institutional changes, both technological and economic. We must "de-carbonize" our energy systems as quickly as feasible by replacing fossil fuels with renewable energy sources that are limitless, benign and harmonious with nature. We especially need to halt the construction of new coal plants, since coal is by far the most polluting and most dangerous source of atmospheric carbon. Wisely utilized, wind power, solar power, tidal power, and geothermal power can provide all the electricity that we require without damaging the biosphere. Since up to a quarter of world carbon emissions result from deforestation, we must reverse the destruction of forests, especially the vital rain forest belt where most species of plants and animals live.

It has recently become quite obvious that significant changes are also needed in the way our economic system is structured. Global warming is intimately related to the gargantuan quantities of energy that our industries devour to provide the levels of consumption that many of us have learned to expect. From a Buddhist perspective, a sane and sustainable economy would be governed by the principle of sufficiency: the key to happiness is content-ment rather than an ever-increasing abundance of goods. The compulsion to consume more and more is an expres-sion of craving, the very thing the Buddha pinpointed as the root cause of suffering.

Instead of an economy that emphasizes profit and requires perpetual growth to avoid collapse, we need to move together towards an economy that provides a satis-factory standard of living for everyone while allowing us to develop our full (including spiritual) potential in harmony with the biosphere that sustains and nurtures all beings, including future generations. If political leaders are unable to recognize the urgency of our global crisis, or unwilling to put the long-term good of humankind above the short-term benefit of fossil-fuel corporations, we may need to chal-lenge them with sustained campaigns of citizen action.

Dr James Hansen of NASA and other climatolo-gists have recently defined the precise targets needed to prevent global warming from reaching catastrophic "tipping points." For human civilization to be sustainable, the safe level of carbon dioxide in the atmosphere is no more than 350 parts per million (ppm). This target has been endorsed by the Dalai Lama, along with other Nobel laureates and distinguished scientists. Our current situa-tion is particularly worrisome in that the present level is already 387 ppm, and has been rising at 2 ppm per year. We are challenged not only to reduce carbon emissions, but also to remove large quantities of carbon gas already present in the atmosphere.

As signatories to this statement of Buddhist principles, we acknowledge the urgent challenge of climate change. We join with the Dalai Lama in endorsing the 350 ppm target. In accordance with Buddhist teachings, we accept our individual and collective responsibility to do whatever we can to meet this target, including (but not limited to) the personal and social responses outlined above.

We have a brief window of opportunity to take action, to preserve humanity from imminent disaster and to assist the survival of the many diverse and beautiful forms of life on Earth. Future generations, and the other species that share the biosphere with us, have no voice to ask for our compassion, wisdom, and leadership. We must listen to their silence. We must be their voice, too, and act on their behalf.

1. According to this Buddhist Declaration, we must reduce our "carbon footprint." What do you think this means?

2. The Dalai Lama, along with distinguished scientists, maintains that human civilization on Earth will not be sustainable if the level of carbon dioxide in the atmosphere exceeds 350 parts per million (ppm). Since the present level has already reached 387 ppm and has been rising at 2 ppm per year, how must our lifestyles change in order to avert disaster?

"HINDU DECLARATION ON CLIMATE CHANGE," FROM HINDU PRESS INTERNATIONAL, DECEMBER 7, 2009

PRESENTED FOR CONSIDERATION TO THE CONVOCATION OF HINDU SPIRITUAL LEADERS

Parliament of the World's Religions, Melbourne, Australia, December 8, 2009

Earth, in which the seas, the rivers and many waters lie, from which arise foods and fields of grain, abode to all that breathes and moves, may She confer on us Her finest yield. Bhumi Suktam, Atharva Veda xii.1.3

The Hindu tradition understands that man is not separate from nature, that we are linked by spiritual, psychological and physical bonds with the elements around us. Knowing that the Divine is present everywhere and in all things, Hindus strive to do no harm. We hold a deep reverence for life and an awareness that the great forces of nature—the earth, the water, the fire, the air and space—as well as all the various orders of life, including plants and trees, forests and animals, are bound to each other within life's cosmic web.

Our beloved Earth, so touchingly looked upon as the Universal Mother, has nurtured mankind through millions of years of growth and evolution. Now centuries of rapacious exploitation of the planet have caught up with us, and a radical change in our relationship with nature is no longer an option. It is a matter of survival. We cannot continue to destroy nature without also destroying ourselves. The dire problems besetting our world—war, disease, poverty and hunger—will all be magnified many fold by the predicted impacts of climate change.

The nations of the world have yet to agree upon a plan to ameliorate man's contribution to this complex change. This is largely due to powerful forces in some nations which oppose any such attempt, challenging the very concept that unnatural climate change is occurring. Hindus everywhere should work toward an international consensus. Humanity's very survival depends upon our capacity to make a major transition of consciousness, equal in significance to earlier transitions from nomadic to agricultural, agricultural to industrial and industrial to technological. We must transit to complementarity in place of competition, convergence in place of conflict, holism in place of hedonism, optimization in place of maxi-mization. We must, in short, move rapidly toward a global consciousness that replaces the present fractured and fragmented consciousness of the human race.

Mahatma Gandhi urged, "You must be the change you wish to see in the world." If alive today, he would call upon Hindus to set the example, to change our lifestyle, to simplify our needs and restrain our desires. As one sixth of the human family, Hindus can have a tremendous impact. We can and should take the lead in Earth-friendly living, personal frugality, lower power consumption, alter-native energy, sustainable food production and vegetari-anism, as well as in evolving technologies that positively address our shared plight. Hindus recognize that it may be too late to avert drastic climate change. Thus, in the spirit of vasudhaiva kutumbakam, "the whole world is one family," Hindus encourage the world to be prepared to respond with compassion to such calamitous challenges as population displacement, food and water shortage, catastrophic weather and rampant disease.

Sanatana Dharma envisions the vastness of God's manifestation and the immense cycles of time in which it is perfectly created, preserved and destroyed, again and again, every dissolution being the preamble to the next creative impulse. Notwithstanding this spiritual reassurance, Hindus still know we must do all that is humanly possible to protect the Earth and her resources for the present as well as future generations.

1. What do you think Mahatma Gandhi meant when he urged, "You must be the change you wish to see in the world"?

EXCERPT FROM *THE REAL GLOBAL WARMING DISASTER: IS THE OBSESSION WITH 'CLIMATE CHANGE' TURNING OUT TO BE THE MOST COSTLY SCIENTIFIC BLUNDER IN HISTORY?* BY CHRISTOPHER BOOKER, FROM CONTINUUM INTERNATIONAL PUBLISHING, USED BY PERMISSION OF BLOOMSBURY PUBLISHING PLC., 2009

The environmentalist narrative had much in common with the Marxist version it for so many people replaced. It divided the world into the exploiters and the exploited. It identified many of the same 'enemies', the power of America and of multi-national corporations, particularly those involved in oil and energy. It saw the rich nations of the world, led by the U.S., living at the expense of the poor. And above all it provided for its adherents the heady sense of being caught up in a great idealistic cause, aimed no longer just at freeing the world from the evils of capitalism but at something more cosmic altogether, saving nothing less than the entire planet fro the greed ad selfishness of humanity.

It had often been observed that Marxism had many parallels with the more extreme forms of organized religion. It similarly had its revered prophets and 'sacred texts'; its dogmatic explanations for everything; its intensely moralistic view of the world; and above all its capacity to inspire its followers to a kind of righteous fanaticism, convinced that it was their destiny to save mankind from those 'heretics' and 'unbelievers' who did not share their world-saving creed.

One of the first people to note that the belief in saving the planet from global warming had also come to display many of the characteristics of a secular religion was the novelist Michael Crichton in 2004, but by 2009 such an observation had become commonplace. The true believers in global warming similarly exhibited a moralistic fanaticism, justified by the transcendent importance of their cause. The basic narrative by which they lived was one familiar from the history of religious sects down the ages, the conviction that the end of the world was nigh, thanks to the wickedness of mankind, and could only be saved if humanity acknowledged its sins and went through a profound change of behavior.

The vision of the coming apocalypse conjured up their prophets, such as Al Gore and James Hansen, and confirmed by those 'sacred texts' handed down by the IPCC, had much in common with ancient myths and Biblical tales of the world being visited with 'extreme weather events', plagues, fires, mighty winds and above all floods so immense that whole cities would vanish below their waves

But all this, of course, was dressed up in new and very different language, deriving its authority not from invocations of the wrath of the Almighty but for that ultimate source of authority in the modern age, the pronouncements from on high of 'science' and 'scientists'.

The only problem was that even the scientists had to rest their prophecies of the future not on absolute and provable scientific certainty, such as governs the workings of the law of gravity, but on belief. And here the scientists themselves had to look to a higher authority on which to base their certainties: namely the predictions made by those terrifyingly powerful computer models which they themselves had programmed.

No theme has run more consistently through the story told in this book than the quasi-religious faith shown in the power of computer models to replicate the complex workings of the earth's climate and to predict what it might be doing in 10, 20, 50, 100 years time. The whole of the global warming scare has ultimately centered on this reverence for the computer model. It stands at the heart of the story like some mysterious fetish at the center of a jungle learning, attended by those modern versions of witch doctors who are the consecrated interpreters of its oracular powers.

The trouble is that those oracular projections rely only on what has been fed into the model by the same witch doctors in the first place. They see in the smoke which emerges from their Delphic caverns only those teasing images which arise from the oils and incense and herbs they themselves have placed on the fire. And ultimately they cannot resolve those teasing images into certainty, because predicting the climate 100 years ahead is such a complex task that they cannot know what magical ingredients they may inadvertently have left out of the mixture.

1. Do you agree with Christopher Booker that true believers in global warming are fanatics, carried away by the moral importance of their cause?

2. How would you characterize Booker's opinion about scientists who believe in global warming, and their "reverence" for their computer models?

CHAPTER 6

WHAT CAN WE DO ABOUT CLIMATE CHANGE?

W hat can we do now to stop the effects of climate change? The most obvious and immediate answer to this question is to reduce the burning of fossil fuels, meaning oil, gas, and coal, as much as humanly possible. But what if humanity's addiction to fossil fuels is too strong for this solution to work? What if it turns out that drastically cutting back our use of these resources enough to stop a disastrous rise in global temperatures is just not possible? Are we then doomed as a species?

In response to the above questions, some people, such as Canadian climate scientist David Keith, have been exploring various technological fixes for an overheated planet. This approach to dealing with climate change is known as "geoengineering." While some scientists state that these ideas may offer a realistic way to cool the earth, other scientists warn that any attempt to alter the climate could backfire and result in a global catastrophe.

According to journalist Elizabeth Kolbert, who produced an award-winning series on climate change, geoengineering sounds like a science-fiction story that will end badly. Indeed, research reports published by the National Academy of Sciences warn that some geoengineering could prove to be beneficial to the Earth—while under-researched and extreme geoengineering could destroy our planet as we know it.

The chapter ends with a quite different "solution." Following a request by Congress to deal with steadily rising sea levels, the Federal Emergency Management Agency (FEMA) is struggling to deal with our new reality.

EXCERPT FROM "A REPORTER'S FIELD NOTES ON THE COVERAGE OF CLIMATE CHANGE," FROM *YALE ENVIRONMENT 360*, MARCH 11, 2009

For nearly a decade, *The New Yorker*'s Elizabeth Kolbert has been reporting on climate change. In an interview with Yale Environment 360, she talked about the responsibility of both the media and scientists to better inform the public about the realities of a warming world.

As a journalist, Elizabeth Kolbert has played a major role in trying to bring the issue of climate change to the attention of the U.S. public. Her award-winning series on climate change in *The New Yorker* in 2005 became the basis for her influential book, *Field Notes From a Catastrophe*, and she has traveled from Greenland to Alaska to the Netherlands reporting on the emerging impacts of global warming.

In an interview with *Yale Environment 360* editor Roger Cohn, Kolbert discussed a wide range of issues: how the media and scientists are both responsible for the lack of public understanding on climate change; the Obama administration's chances of passing climate-related legislation; and the prospects of geoengineering the planet to mitigate the effects of warming. On whether there is a moral or ethical dimension to this issue, she observed, "It seems to me that if there's not a moral dimension to potentially leaving a totally impoverished planet to future generations, all future generations, I don't know what would be."

Yale Environment 360: Surveys show that most Americans don't actually know that much about climate change and don't consider it much of a priority in terms of issues that need action or attention. Why do you think that's true? And related to that, how good a job has the media done in conveying the issue to the public?

Elizabeth Kolbert: I think the reason it doesn't register in the polls is partly just due to the nature of the problem. I mean, if you look at polls, you see right now, for example, that obviously the economy is just through the roof. So whatever is going on at that particular moment that is really affecting people's lives, that's what ranks high in the polls. And climate change has often been described as a slow-moving catastrophe, and it's precisely the kind of issue that once you actually really feel the dire effects in your own life, then it's way too late. That's what the science tells us and what scientists have been telling us for 25 years now really. So it's a very, very difficult problem for the political system to deal with.

I went to interview John McCain, and he made this point. He was very honest and it was back in the straight-talking John McCain days, where he said, "It's very unclear whether our political system can deal with a problem like this because usually we wait for a crisis and then we deal with the crisis, and that's just not the way climate change works. You can't deal with it once the crisis hits."

I think that's one of the reasons that it doesn't register very high in polls as a concern — it's just not in people's faces all the time right now. So it really is the obligation, you could argue, of the media and also of the political system, to put it there. And the political system has been very consciously ignoring the problem for a long time now, eight years of really trying to suppress discussion of climate change and reports about climate change. So I think that also contributes to the public sense of "I don't have to worry about that," because they're not hearing people talking about it in Washington. And now that is changing to a certain extent.

I think that the media has contributed to the general sense of it not being an urgent problem because it's not the lead story of the paper every day. It's a very hard issue for the media to deal with precisely because the news business is about news — it's about something that happened yesterday. And global warming is just happening all around us all the time, and it's going to continue to happen and it doesn't present itself as news very often.

e360: But why has the media not done more to get it out there? Is it more than just the headline issue?

Kolbert: Well, look, the Australians are now having a terrible heat wave, and they're having a terrible drought. And it's just generally agreed that they're having a long-term drought, and that this is climate change, a climate change signal. They're really in dire straits. They have no water in parts of the country that used to be significant agricultural areas, the Murray-Darling Basin. And it has woken the Australians up pretty quickly, and there's a lot of coverage on climate change issues if you are reading the Australian media.

So unfortunately, I think it does take something that's very, very palpable, really affecting people's lives. And as I say, precisely the message that scientists have been trying to give us is, do not wait until that drought hits you, because that's too late.

e360: You did your series in *The New Yorker* on global warming in 2005 and that became the basis of your book *Field Notes From a Catastrophe*. But you had actually been writing about global warming even before that series. How was it that you, who came not out of the history of writing about environmental issues but had written about New York politics, how was it you came to focus on this issue?

Kolbert: I just really was interested in it and thought that even I, who read the papers every day, didn't really have a very clear sense of what was going on. Even at that point, it was basically 12 years or whatever after [NASA's] Jim Hansen had announced that we can see evidence of global warming. He was 99 percent sure that we were seeing global warming happening. But we were just sort of in this fog. Nothing was happening. It wasn't really being talked about. And so, in part to satisfy my own interest of what was going on, I set out to write a piece.

e360: What was the first story you did on global warming?

Kolbert: Well, a couple of years earlier, I had gone up to an ice-coring operation in the middle of Greenland, which was a very, very eye-opening experience. It's now become sort of a standard line in global warming coverage to note that we're seeing the beginnings of the melting of the Greenland ice sheet, which could eventually raise sea levels by 20 feet. And it seems perplexing if you've never seen the ice sheet, because like, what could raise sea levels globally by 20 feet? When you actually stand on top of almost 11,000 feet of ice, it becomes more comprehensible. It's such an amazing place, and you realize how startling the world is and how very contingent and fragile the conditions that we live under are. There's a lot of water locked up in that ice sheet. That's a function of having been through an Ice Age not that long ago in geological terms, and we're sort of still living off of the ends of that Ice Age. And if you start pushing things too far in one direction, you're going to change the planet very, very radically. And it really struck me in ways that I hadn't really comprehended before when I went up to the top of the ice sheet. So that had a big effect on me. It's still one of my favorite places in the world, just to be on top of the Greenland ice sheet.

e360: We've talked about journalists and generally the challenges in conveying this issue to the public. But what about scientists? I mean, scientists have a responsibility to get their information out to the public whether it's through the media or through their own writings and work. How good a job do you think they have done in conveying this whole issue?

Kolbert: Oh, I don't think they've done a good job. They have some of the same problems that journalists have, which is that scientists are interested in introducing something new in their work. They want new results, new information. They want to break new ground. They need to do that to get funding, really. And global warming, the fact that global warming is happening, that is really old news in scientific circles. It's just a settled question in scientific circles. So scientists moved on to other issues having to do with climate change...

e360: But not whether it exists?

Kolbert: No, absolutely not. That would be considered — you'd just be laughed at in a scientific discussion. But that message really never reached the public, and you could argue that that's the journalists' fault, and I do fault journalists for that. But I also fault scientists because they sort of have just left things to the journalists. And now that we've sort of moved to a new stage of the debate, a policy debate, they're not going to be involved in that either. They're going to leave that to the economists or to the political scientists.

And I think that's a big mistake because when you read a lot of economic analyses of climate change, you are struck with a very worrisome sense that the economists don't understand the science, don't appreciate the gravity of the situation. And they don't seem to be factoring in the notion of we're not talking here about small, inconvenient changes that are not worth changing our lifestyle to avoid. We're talking about a desolate planet, not really in that long a time, okay?

In terms of generations that we will touch, certainly our grandchildren will be facing a very, very bleak future if we just sit on our hands for not that much longer. So I really urge scientists to make their voices heard, and I think there's a certain moral urgency to that — and I think some scientists feel that way.

e360: There have been scientists who have been out there — James Hansen, most publicly and most notably — trying to get the message out in every way they can. But when this message does get out, there is some public reaction that these scientists are like Chicken Little — you know, the sky is falling.

Kolbert: Right.

e360: If you turn on the TV news, the weathermen are making global warming jokes, saying, "This isn't global warming. Hey, who said anything about global warming? It's cold today." There's still this reaction, even when the facts are presented to them.

Kolbert: Absolutely. This is a total system failure, okay? We're not talking about an isolated little problem, and that's the problem. It's a total system failure that we're in this situation and it's a total system failure that we can't seem to steer away even when the evidence is absolutely overwhelming that we better do something.

It gets back to this issue of whether the public believes in science, which, to be honest, we do not. You can still find a lot of people who don't believe in evolution, okay? So we're talking about a country that has a very lax relationship to science. And what you need in order to grapple meaningfully with global warming is to believe that this is not a speculative thing. This is the way geophysics work, and we have established that very clearly both in a laboratory setting and on the ground — and we need to take very seriously these predictions.

I mean, Freeman Dyson has done a tremendous amount of damage saying, "I don't believe models. We can't model this." Well, we actually can model it very accurately, it turns out. And we're talking about very fundamental science. It's not a very complicated science. And so when you have people like that out there sort of blowing smoke, really, I would say, it is hard for the public to know what to do. So I think scientists need to try to convey how virtually unanimous this consensus is, because otherwise people will just believe that the science is fuzzy or foggy.

e360: Well, we now have a new administration that certainly has come into office with very different ideas about this issue and the urgency of dealing with it than the previous administration. What do you see as the prospects for some real meaningful action on climate change by the U.S. and by the world community?

Kolbert: Well, I think it's going to be really hard. I think Obama's platform was very ambitious. He has a good plan put together by good people, but to translate that into a legislative action is going to be very, very difficult because of the way that our system can be held hostage by a minority. My fear is that in order to get something through Congress, it will be so watered down as to be meaningless.

But Obama has a lot of people around him who know a lot more than I do about climate change and are very passionately concerned about this issue and know what needs to be done to have a meaningful effect. So we'll see whether they can prevent that sort of inevitable watering down.

e360: What is it that the U.S. needs to do that shouldn't be watered down?

Kolbert: What the U.S. needs to do — and it's like so simple as to be almost laughable — is it needs to start bringing its emissions down. We just need to do that virtually immediately, and we need some intermediate targets, and we need some long-term targets. Obama's long-term target was 2050 — that's when we're going to have an 80 percent reduction in CO_2. Well, you can't get that all in 2045. You need to start yesterday...

If we start on a downward trajectory, we will be doing the right thing. We need to start turning this line that's sloping upward — it needs to peak tomorrow and then start turning downward. And if we did that, or if you've just committed to doing that, we would send a very strong signal to the world that a new era genuinely was beginning. You can yak all you want about green jobs, about green stimulus, blah-blah-blah. But until you actually turn emissions down, it's pretty meaningless.

e360: Do you think that there is a moral and ethical dimension to the issue of climate change?

Kolbert: Yeah. Well, I'm no moral philosopher, but it seems to me in that if there's not a moral dimension to potentially leaving a totally impoverished planet to future generations, all future generations, I don't know what would be.

These are changes that last thousands of years. They're not things that you could turn around. What we've done to the oceans, for example, in terms of adding CO_2 or, really, carbonic acid to the oceans, changing the chemistry of the oceans. That is irreversible for on the order of 10,000 years, okay? So we're talking about, basically, for all intents and purposes, forever... What is our ethical obligation if not to hand off a planet that's habitable? I can't really see a higher ethical obligation.

e360: There's increasing talk recently about the need to proceed with adaptation strategies to find ways to geo-engineer or manipulate things on Earth to compensate or reduce the impact of climate change. What do you think about that and the prospects of that?

Kolbert: Well, I think that you do hear more and more conversation about geoengineering, absolutely. A lot of people are thinking about it, but I have personally yet to hear a credible sort of scheme. All these things so far that people have come up with have significant damaging properties of their own. What you're talking about, you're talking about trying to block sunlight basically. You're literally talking about trying to have less sunlight reach the Earth. That's pretty serious. And then you have to think about if you keep adding CO_2 to the atmosphere, then you have to block more and more sunlight, so eventually it really gets pretty ugly.

I think that some emergency measures will have to be taken to, for example, prevent Greenland from melting. But it has to be in concert with bringing emissions down, because otherwise you're just in this kind of arms race of combating more and more CO_2. You're forcing the climate in one direction basically, and then you have to force it back in another direction. It sort of comes to this game of tug-of-war, and you could see how that would really get out of control.

And I should also point out that there's a U.N. treaty that prevents us from screwing around with the weather, and there are a lot of international impediments. You can't just go up there, one country, and shoot something into the upper atmosphere that will have a global effect. You need international cooperation on that too. And it seems like the fact that we're willing to contemplate these things as opposed to taking the steps we already know how to do to reduce CO_2 emissions — which have to do with such simple things as mass transit systems — that we'd rather totally change the atmosphere in a new way strikes me as kind of this techno dream we've been living in for a hundred years now or whatever. And it seems to me this is like a bad science-fiction story, and you kind of know where that one's going to end.

e360: You've covered the science of this, covered the politics of it. How optimistic are you that we're going to actually do what needs to be done to deal with this?

Kolbert: Well, I'm not at all optimistic. I do see a lot of energy in Washington from very smart and committed people, so that's a very helpful sign. But I don't see any sign as a society that we're really willing to do what needs to be done.

That being said, I think that people surprise you, and I'm hoping to be surprised. I mean, I was one of those people who was pessimistic about Obama, the prospect of electing a black president seemed to be not that plausible, and here we are today. So things do happen that surprise you. And I'm hoping to be surprised over the next four years and to see some really serious legislative action.

1. According to Elizabeth Kolbert, how has the media contributed to Americans' seeming lack of concern about global warming?

2. Why does Kolbert compare the various geoengineering schemes to a bad science-fiction story?

"GEOENGINEERING: THE PROSPECT OF MANIPULATING THE PLANET," BY JEFF GOODELL, FROM *YALE ENVIRONMENT 360*, JANUARY 7, 2009

Although he finds the possibility unsettling, Canadian climate scientist David Keith believes large-scale geo-engineering will eventually be deployed to offset global warming. In an interview with Yale Environment 360, Keith explains to Jeff Goodell why scientists must begin researching an "emergency response strategy" for cooling an overheated planet.

Geoengineering, which is usually defined as the deliberate, large-scale manipulation of the earth's climate to offset the impact of greenhouse gas emissions, has long been a taboo subject among top climate scientists and policymakers. At first glance, the whole idea reeks of technological hubris ("It's the Frankenplanet solution," as one beltway environmentalist put it).

And yet, because of our failure to cut global green-house gas emissions, as well as growing alarm about how quickly our climate is changing, the taboo is fading. In 2006, Paul Crutzen, who won a Nobel Prize for his work on ozone chemistry, published a widely read paper that basi-cally announced that geoengineering might be needed as a last resort against global warming. Ralph Cicerone, the head of the U.S. Academy of Sciences, has also given the idea cautionary support. Last fall, the British Royal Society launched an in-depth study to explore various methods and potential risks. All this activity might be best seen less as hubris than desperation.

Geoengineering is really a catchall term that applies to two very different ideas: one is carbon engineering, which covers everything from dumping iron in the ocean to stimulate plankton blooms to building stand-alone scrubbers that can pull CO_2 out of the atmosphere. The second is albedo engineering, which refers to technologies that might be used to cool the planet by changing the earth's albedo (i.e., reflectivity) by creating what amount to artificial volcanoes that shoot tiny particles into the stratosphere, for example, or building cloud-generation machines. Carbon engineering is the least controversial of the two approaches, in part because it's slow-acting and essentially mimics the earth's natural carbon cycle (you could argue that reforestation is a form of carbon engineering). In contrast, albedo engineering — or "climate intervention," as some scientists now prefer to call it — is a far more ethically fraught option that might be deployed only if we get into a climate emergency and need to cool the earth in a hurry.

The technological, political, and moral complexities of all this are profound, and few scientists have given them more consideration than David Keith, who holds the Canada Research Chair in Energy and the Environment at the University of Calgary. Although Keith spends most of his time working on carbon capture and storage (he's currently overseeing a large CCS demonstration program in Canada), he has been thinking and writing about geoengineering for more than 20 years. At a recent meeting of the American Geophysical Union in San Francisco, where Keith delivered a talk called "Climate Engineering and Climate Stabilization," I interviewed him for *Yale Environment 360* and asked about some of the controversies and complexities of geoengineering.

Yale Environment 360: Geoengineering has long been dismissed as a crazy and dangerous idea. But in your talk yesterday you said that geoengineering should be part of "our toolbox" to use as a response to global warming. Why?

David Keith: The central argument has to do with the uncertainty that has persisted for decades and still does about just how bad the climate problem is. It comes down to a parameter that climate scientists call "climate sensi-tivity" — how much the climate will warm if we, say, double the amount of CO_2 in the air. And the answer is thatбs still uncertain by factors of two or three, which is just gigantic. So if we are very lucky, it might be that we could double or triple the amount of CO_2 in the air and have relatively small climate change, some of which might be beneficial.

On the flip side, if we're unlucky, we might see 5 or 6 degrees [Celsius] globally — and you can double that if you're in the middle of a mid-latitude continent — which is just stunning. That's as big as the change between the glacial and the interglacial state and that would certainly, over a few hundred years, melt big sections of the ice caps. It's really quite horrific stuff. And we don't know which of those two it is, and we're not going to know in time.

So we're making decisions every day by continuing to put CO_2 in the air — decisions that we cannot easily reverse. And so the culmination of the CO_2 in the air, and that uncertainty about how dangerous it is, that means you need a backup plan.

e360: One of the first things that comes up in many peo-ple's minds when they think about geoengineering is the idea of moral hazard. As you know better than anyone, the need to cut emissions to deal with global warming is one of the hardest tasks human beings have ever set their shoulders to, and geoengineering is seen by many as a dangerous distraction.

Keith: That's a really hard question, and I have different views depending on which side of the bed I get up on in the morning. I guess if youʼre a total rationalist, the answer is we certainly should *not* put all of our efforts into cutting emissions. We should put most of our current money and work into cutting emissions, but we do need to figure out what to do in this worst case scenario. So you need to put lots of effort into making sure you donʼt have house fires, but you also need to have a plan in case you do have a house fire.

But of course in the real world, where we don't have a rational, single planner, it's perfectly legitimate to worry that conversations about this will cause people to be less active in cutting emissions. And I should say personally, I do worry about this.

But I don't think science does well by hiding things. Einstein has a beautiful quote that says, "It's a privilege to seek for truth, but that privilege implies also a duty and that duty is to show all the truth that you find." And the idea that scientific elite will try to bottle it up and hide it from the masses so the masses don't get some ideas about how we might actually deal with the problem is really reprehensible — and not one that's really going to produce good policy anyway.

So I think we have to talk about it seriously. What we need is to get out of the blogsphere hype-mode that it's currently in, and get a real, not necessarily gigantic, but real research program going that will normalize work on geoengineering.

e360: What are the environmental risks associated with geoengineering that you think are most serious?

Keith: Well, the risks depend partly on what methods you actually use doing the geoengineering. If you put sulfur in the stratosphere, there›s some possibility you›ll decrease the amount of ozone in the stratosphere because we›ve observed that with volcanoes and sulfur in the stratosphere. And if you put some advanced engineered particles in the stratosphere like I›ve spent some time thinking about, it might be those particles have some completely unexpected environmental impact that we don›t know about. After all, there's a painfully long history of us doing engineering interventions in the earth's systems to solve one problem, and we just end up creating another problem. But despite that history, that's not an excuse for doing nothing.

Just let me say one more thing this moral hazard question. There are lots of things we talk about in the climate game that are pernicious, and that gave people a false sense of security — and it is by no means clear that this is the scariest one. When you buy an airline ticket, you can now check a box that buys you some carbon offsets that makes it seem like your aircraft flight is carbon neutral. That's no more true than it was true that when you bought indulgences from the Catholic Church in the good old days that you really had not sinned. There is no technology right now that truly offsets the carbon emissions in an airplane flight — which after all stays in the atmosphere for millennia.

And this pernicious idea that the problem can be easily solved, which is sometimes hyped by people in the green power industry who want to make us think that we can solve this problem and get rich all at the same time, is probably more destructive — in terms of weakening people's realizations of how serious the problem is and how much we really have to do — than these conversations about geoengineering.

e360: One of the things that distinguishes you from other scientists who have been talking about geoengineering is that you think this can be a way to save ecosystems like the Arctic — that there is an environmental component to this. *[Ed. Note: Changing the albedo in the Arctic, perhaps by increasing cloud cover above the region or shooting particles in the atmosphere, could in theory stop or even reverse the ice melt.]*

Keith: Well that's certainly my main motivation. I don't think that civilization is at stake with global warming. But I think that loss of the natural world we care about *is* at stake. To amplify that, there are things that can really threaten human civilization. And those things, in my view, are things like large-scale war with chemical or biological weapons. Those are things we should be very worried about, because, after all, we still live in a world where the only ultimate way to actually settle disputes between nation states is by war. And war, with the kind of technologies we now have, is really unacceptable. And I think that that is truly a civilization-wrecking outcome.

As much as I sometimes wish we could find a civilization-wrecking outcome from global warming, because that would force people to cut emissions very quickly, I don't believe there is one. I think humans are amazingly adaptable and have amazing powers of isolating themselves from the environment by their technology, and those powers are not going to go away. And even human wants are very adaptable. So while I'm not claiming there won't be bad impacts from global warming — of course there will be, I spent my whole lifetime writing on that topic — I don't see it as a civilizational threat.

On the other hand, I do see the combination of very, very rapid warming — such as the Earth has not seen perhaps for 55 million years or even longer — combined with the other forces on the natural world, including human appropriation of land and all the different ways we're chopping up the natural environment, could really be devastating for the natural world that lots of us love. And I think that is one of the reasons to take this seriously.

e360: I know you've thought a lot about what a geoengineering research program should look like. But a lot of people would argue that starting a research program on this begins the slippery slope towards deployment — you don't research these kinds of problems and then let the technology sit on the shelf. Do you agree?

Keith: I think there are some elements to that that make sense. But what's the alternative? So are we going to not research it ... and then what's going to happen if we find that the climate sensitivity actually is six degrees and we get to a point where we have 550 ppm [parts per million] CO_2 in the air and Greenland is melting? Then what's going to happen is we're going to do it anyway, even if we haven't done research. We're going to do it chaotically and quickly and stupidly. Because it is not true that if we don't do the research, this will never happen.

e360: When we were talking earlier today you said that you thought we will eventually do this, that we will eventually geoengineer the planet. Is there a kind of inevitability to this, do you see it as part of the arc of human progress?

Keith: Yeah, I think it's true. It's not something I necessarily want to see. But I think unless humans have some war that sets back human civilization, we will grow into doing a kind of planetary management. I think we'll end up being in the gardening business with this planet.

But I think we'd be better to do that much slower rather than quicker. And my hope would be we cut emissions enough that we don't need to geoengineer in the short-term, because I think that while technically we might be able to do this, humans are probably morally unready, or society is unready, to figure out how they'd use the power that comes from our technology to manipulate the planet.

One glib way to think about this is to imagine that space aliens come down and land on the White House lawn or wherever — maybe they'll choose to land in Kenya — and they give us some magic tools for controlling the climate, including a box that has a knob for global temperature and a knob for CO_2 concentration. If that happened right now, you can imagine people fighting wars over the place to set the knobs, because we have no global government that's able to figure out what the right answer is. And I don't think obviously that scenario is likely to happen. But the fact is human-sized technology is gradually building us the tools to have that level of control over the climate. And not necessarily in 20 years, but in 100 years, I think it's very likely we'll have the power to determine the global climate.

And the point is, we should start thinking about what that means now — what it means in moral and political terms — so we can build institutions that are able to effectively manage this technology. We have seen time and time again with email and cell phones that human technology often moves quicker than our social systems can adapt.

But does that mean we should slow down technological progress? Maybe yes. In some cases, clearly yes. But in a case like this, I don't think you can say that, because we're actually putting CO_2 in the air. We need an emergency response strategy.

1. Why does David Keith believe we should certainly consider certain types of geoengineering to mitigate the effects of global warming?

2. Why does Keith not see global warming as a civilizational threat?

"THERE'S A GOOD AND A BAD WAY TO 'GEOENGINEER' THE PLANET," BY CRAIG WELCH/*NATIONAL GEOGRAPHIC CREATIVE*, FEBRUARY 9, 2015

Fighting climate change by pulling CO_2 out of the atmosphere makes sense, an expert committee says. Blocking the sun, not so much.

Developing the technology to suck planet-warming carbon dioxide back out of the atmosphere is an expensive but promising approach that may be necessary to help prevent the worst effects of climate change, according to the first of two reports released this morning by the research arm of the National Academy of Sciences.

But according to the second report, proposals to cool the planet on the cheap by reflecting sunlight are so risky that even serious study of them should be undertaken only in preparation for an emergency.

Together the two reports from the National Research Council (NRC) offer the most comprehensive U.S. examination yet of "geoengineering"—the intentional intervening in the climate system in an attempt to forestall some of the impact of global warming.

"The world is in a very tough situation, and there's no magic bullet here, unfortunately," said Paul Falkowski, a biochemistry professor at Rutgers University, who worked on the reports.

An NRC committee of experts from across disciplines was asked by several U.S. government science and intelligence agencies to evaluate geoengineering proposals. The ideas range from anodyne (planting trees to capture CO_2) to potentially alarming (injecting sulfate particles or other aerosols into the atmosphere to reflect sunlight and cool the planet).

Committee members were blunt in their first recommendation: The world should focus first and foremost on curbing fossil fuel emissions rather than on any kind of geoengineering.

"I think it's going to be easier and cheaper to avoid making a mess than it will be to make a mess and then try to clean it up later" said committee member Ken Caldeira, a climate scientist at Stanford University's Carnegie Institution for Science. "If we end up having to build a fix that's on the scale of our energy system, why not just retool our energy system?"

Six years after a report from the Royal Society in the United Kingdom reached many of the same conclusions, the American scientists decided to issue two reports—to distinguish as forcefully as they could between two very different approaches that for years have been lumped together under the heading "geoengineering."

The first, CO_2 removal, the committee characterized as worthy and "almost inevitable." The second, using aerosols or other means to reflect solar radiation, would be "irrational and irresponsible" if done as anything but a last-ditch effort to prevent a global famine or other emergency.

"We were clearly trying to send a message that we didn't want to paint CO_2 removal with the same geoengineering label," said committee member Steve Fetter, associate provost at the University of Maryland's School of Public Policy.

REMOVING CO_2

Even the Intergovernmental Panel on Climate Change (IPCC) has suggested in its most recent report that CO_2 at 400 parts per million and rising, the world seems likely to overshoot the target of 450 parts per million needed to kept the global average temperature from rising more than 2 degrees Celsius (3.6 degrees Fahrenheit)—a level many scientists consider a danger threshold.

IPCC scenarios that avoid dangerous climate change typically assume that we'll reduce CO_2 emissions to zero and develop a way of reducing atmospheric CO_2 by the second half of this century.

There are various ideas about how to do that. The simplest is planting forests, which store CO2 in wood and soil as they grow. Another is burning wood or other plant matter for energy, then capturing and burying the CO2 before it exits the smokestack. A third idea is to develop chemical scrubbers, like the ones used to purify air on submarines, that remove CO_2 directly from the air.

"I personally think it will be necessary," Fetter said, meaning CO_2 removal in general. "CO_2 concentrations already are too high and increasing, and it's hard to see a realistic scenario in which we can limit and stabilize greenhouse gases at a level that doesn't pose a threat without employing some form of CO_2 removal."

The problem, he said, is that "all the things we can do that are cheap, like planting trees, are limited in their capacity."

CO_2 removal is also not a quick fix. The volume required to make a difference would be enormous— humans now emit more than 36 billion metric tons of

CO_2 a year—and the benefits would take a long time to appear. At the moment, the NRC report concluded, no one approach to CO_2 removal can be relied upon to make a huge dent without enormous front-end costs.

"You really need to spread your bets over a variety of techniques," said committee member Scott Doney, a marine geochemist at Woods Hole Oceanographic Institution.

Another reason that CO_2 removal would almost certainly become necessary is that some parts of the energy system may use fossil fuels for a long time to come.

"It's really hard, for example, to make carbon-net-zero airplanes," said committee member Granger Morgan, a professor of engineering and public policy at Carnegie Mellon University. "But if you can scrub CO_2 out of the atmosphere for a reasonable price, that might be a strategy."

BLOCKING THE SUN

The second NRC report released today details the far more fraught idea of increasing the planet's albedo—its reflectivity—so that more sunlight gets bounced back into space.

An example of this approach would be to use high-flying planes to inject sulfate particles into the stratosphere—essentially mimicking the effects of volcanoes such as Mount Pinatubo, whose massive eruption in 1991 cooled the planet by about one degree Fahrenheit.

Though that type of geoengineering would be far cheaper than CO_2 removal, the NRC report said, it would not address the underlying problem: the accumulation of CO_2 in the atmosphere. Nor would it stop the oceans from acidifying as they absorb CO_2.

What's more, any scheme to increase Earth's reflectivity would pose enormous unknown ecological and political risks, the report said. If it were done as an alternative to reducing CO_2 emissions, it would have to be done forever, since catastrophic global warming might ensue if it were halted.

"It's not ready for prime time," said Doney. "The committee strongly recommends not moving forward at this time."

Still, the committee gingerly recommended taking steps toward doing careful research on the topic, calling for a global discussion on setting research parameters.

In an emergency, such as a massive global famine, some way of cooling the planet quickly might be needed to provide a temporary reprieve. Rogue states might also decide to try doing that on their own, which would require that mainstream scientists understand the potential consequences well enough to recommend a response.

"I'm terrified of the idea," said committee member and climate scientist Ray Pierrehumbert of the University of Chicago. "But even if we all think it's a really, really bad idea, there are still good reasons to want to know more."

"DESPAIR IS NOT AN OPTION"

Despite the complexity of the climate problem, several committee members said they remained optimistic.

Falkowski pointed out that technology can, and often has, changed overnight. The time between the drilling of the first oil well and an America with cars and airplanes was only about 60 years, he said, which suggests we're capable of remaking out energy system again in the next 60 years.

"The way I look at it is, Despair is not an option," Pierrehumbert said. "It's going to be really, really hard to avoid 2 degrees of warming. Barring some technological miracle, we'll probably blow right past it. But the really, really bad things start to happen between 2 and 4 degrees, and we still have a pretty good window of avoiding 4 degrees.

"By doing our very, very best," Pierrehumbert said, "and if we do manage to get CO_2 removal going, we might then be able to bring it back down under 2 degrees in a century or so."

1. Which of the two approaches to geoengineering the earth in order to lessen or prevent the impact of global warming makes more sense to you? Why?

"WHAT HAPPENED AFTER CONGRESS PASSED A CLIMATE CHANGE LAW? VERY LITTLE," BY THEODORIC MEYER, FROM PROPUBLICA, OCTOBER 15, 2013

Congress did something unusual last year. It passed a bill that acknowledged that sea levels are rising — i.e., that climate change is happening.

The measure in question, buried near the end of a 584-page transportation funding bill, also required some modest action: That the Federal Emergency Management Agency use "the best available climate science" to figure out how the flood insurance program it administers should handle rising seas.

FEMA's first step was supposed to be to set up an advisory body, the Technical Mapping Advisory Council, that would make recommendations on how the agency could take the effects of climate change into account in its flood insurance maps.

But more than a year later, FEMA hasn't named a single member to the council. Without any members, it has been unable to meet or make any recommendations. In July, the council missed a deadline set out in the law for submitting written recommendations for how the flood insurance program might deal with future risks related to climate change.

FEMA had developed a charter for the council by the end of August and was in the process of finalizing letters to solicit council members, according to the agency. Dan Watson, the FEMA press secretary, said he was unable to provide more up-to-date information because much of the agency's staff has been furloughed under the government shutdown.

Few areas of the federal government are more directly affected by climate change than the flood insurance program and its maps, which determine the premiums that 5.6 million American households pay for flood insurance. The program fell deeply into the red after Hurricane Katrina in 2005 and Hurricane Sandy last year. It's currently $25 billion in debt.

Many of the maps are decades out of date and therefore don't reflect the rise in sea levels since the time they were drawn.

FEMA released a report in June estimating that sea levels will rise an average of four feet by 2100, increasing the portion of the country at high risk of flooding by up to 45 percent. The number of Americans who live in those areas could double by the century's end, according to the report.

The law requires the council to outline steps for improving the "accuracy, general quality, ease of use, and distribution and dissemination" of the maps. Josh Saks, legislative director for the National Wildlife Federation, which pushed for the legislation, said that might include figuring out how to better take into account the way new development along a river, say, worsens flooding for those who live downstream.

Jimi Grande, the senior vice president for federal and political affairs for the National Association of Mutual Insurance Companies, a lobbying group, said the council would "absolutely" help make the flood maps more accurate.

"We need to know what the risks are to have an intelligent conversation as a country" about development in areas that are vulnerable to flooding, he said.

The measure was part of a broader package of reforms to the National Flood Insurance Program that phased out many of the government subsidies that had kept flood insurance premiums artificially cheap for many homeowners. The full-risk rates phased in for many policyholders on Oct. 1, despite vocal protests against them.

An operational mapping advisory council wouldn't fix everything that's wrong with the flood insurance program. As ProPublica has reported, some of the maps FEMA has issued in recent years have been based on outdated, inaccurate data, giving homeowners a misleading impression of flood risk and, in some cases, forcing them to buy insurance when they were not at great risk of flooding.

Taking climate change into account when setting flood insurance rates is also a complex task.

"That's why we put the council in charge," said Saks, from the National Wildlife Federation. "I can read the science and say storms are happening more often, and I can read the numbers and see that sea-level rise is happening. But I'm not an actuary, and I don't know how you then translate that to" setting insurance rates.

The risk-modeling companies that private insurers rely on have struggled to take climate change into account in their models, but they are making progress.

"I wouldn't be too surprised if within the next five years we could credibly start to incorporate climate change into aspects of the modeling," said David F. Smith, the vice president of the model development group at Eqecat, a risk-modeling firm.

Michael B. Gerrard, director of the Center for Climate Change Law at Columbia University, said he wasn't surprised FEMA had been slow in setting up the council.

"It's the rule, rather than the exception, that federal agencies miss the rule-making deadlines" set out in laws, he said. "Often they have to be sued to get back on schedule."

1. Why do you think that the "measure in question," which stipulated that Congress agree that climate change is occurring and that steps need to be taken to manage it, was buried at the end of a long transportation bill?

CONCLUSION

By now, having read the various perspectives on climate change from thoughtful people in the worlds of politics, science, religion, and business, as well as climate activists and environmentalists, you must be aware of the complexity of the whole issue of global warming and how people respond to it. Most people, whatever they think about climate change, are sincere in their beliefs. They have their reasons for believing global warming is either a great danger for humanity, or for denying its existence. Unfortunately, there are still those who, for political reasons or for vested business interests, claim that global warming, if it even exists, is not caused by human activity.

Hopefully, this book has helped you arrive at your own conclusions if you previously had not made up your mind about climate change and a warming world. Scientists predict that global warming will transform our world into a different kind of planet. Even if humans are able to adapt to drastic environmental changes brought about by the changing climate, many thousands of other species, animal as well as plant, will not. If you believe that global warming is real and that it presents the greatest threat that humanity faces in the twenty-first century, it's important to not give in to despair and think that nothing can be done about it.

Before scientists decide to resort to one or another strategy of geoengineering to fix the problem, there are much more practical and less dangerous approaches to attempt first. For example, moving from the use of fossil fuels to solar, wind, and other forms of renewable energy would greatly diminish the emission of greenhouse gases. More widespread use of electric or hybrid vehicles would certainly cut back the spewing of CO2 into the atmosphere. Improving the insulation of buildings would also save energy.

There are many things that you can do if you want to fight global warming. Continue to keep up with the latest developments by reading what scientists, environmentalists, and government officials have to say. Send e-mails or letters to your government representatives, urging them to support legislation aimed at reducing greenhouse gas emissions. Be informed about what climate activists are doing. Consider joining one of the many groups fighting global warming. With each passing day, more and more people in countries all around the world are becoming involved in the effort to fight climate change. This is a big reason for some optimism about the future.

BIBLIOGRAPHY

Aiken, William et al. "The Time to Act Is Now: A Buddhist Declaration on Climate Change." May 14, 2015. Retrieved January 8, 2015 (http://fore.yale.edu/files/Buddhist_Climate_Change_Statement_5-14-15.pdf).

"As NY State Probes Exxon, Oil Giant Targets the Journalists Who Exposed Climate Change Cover-Up." *Democracy Now!*, December 2, 2015. Retrieved April 27, 2016 (http://www.democracynow.org/2015/12/2/as_ny_state_probes_exxon_oil).

Booker, Christopher. *The Real Global Warming Disaster: Is the Obsession with 'Climate Change' Turning Out to Be the Most Costly Scientific Blunder in History?* London: Continuum International Publishing Group, used by permission of Bloomsbury Publishing Plc., 2009.

"Climate Scientist Michael Mann, interviewed by Thom Hartmann on The Big Picture." Transcribed by Sue Nethercott. *Thom Hartmann*, November 10, 2015. Retrieved January 8, 2016 (http://www.thomhartmann.com/blog/2015/11/transcript-understanding-climate-change-conversation-michael-mann-10-november-15).

"Ethics on Film: Discussion of *An Inconvenient Truth.*" Carnegie Council for Ethics in International Affairs. Retrieved April 27, 2016 (https://www.carnegiecouncil.org/education/002/film/reviews/0001.html).

"Freeman Dyson Takes on the Climate Establishment." *Yale Environment 360*, June 4, 2009. Retrieved January 8, 2016 (http://e360.yale.edu/feature/freeman_dyson_takes_on_the_climate_establishment/2151).

Goodell, Jeff. "Geoengineering: The Prospect of Manipulating the Planet: Yale Environment 360 interview with David Keith." *Yale Environment 360*, January 7, 2009. Retrieved January 8, 2016 (http://e360.yale.edu/feature/geoengineering_the_prospect_of_manipulating_the_planet/2107/).

"Hindu Declaration on Climate Change." Presented for Consideration to the Convocation of Hindu Spiritual Leaders Parliament of the World's Religions, Melbourne, Australia, December 8, 2009. Retrieved January 8, 2016 (http://www.hinduismtoday.com/pdf_downloads/hindu-climate-change-declaration.pdf).

"Islamic Declaration on Global Climate Change 2015 International Climate Change Symposium." Islamic Relief Worldwide. Retrieved January 8, 2016 (http://islamicclimatedeclaration.org /islamic-declaration-on-global-climate-change/).

Kirk, Martin. "Us and Them: On Understanding Climate Denialism." Common Dreams, March 9, 2015. Retrieved April 27, 2016 (http://www.commondreams.org/views/2015/03/19 /us-and-them-understanding-climate-denialism).

Lewis, Avi and Rajiv Sicora. "Why Most of What You Think You Know About the Paris Climate Deal is Wrong: An Annotated News Story." Common Dreams, December 20, 2015. Retrieved January 8, 2016 (http://www.commondreams.org /views/2015/12/19/why-most-what-you-think-you-know-about -paris-climate-deal-wrong-annotated-news).

McCauley, Lauren. "More Than Exxon: Big Oil Companies for Years Shared Damning Climate Research." Common Dreams, December 22, 2015. Retrieved January 8, 2016 (http://www. commondreams.org/news/2015/12/22/more-exxon-big-oil -companies-years-shared-damning-climate-research).

Meyer, Theodoric. "What Happened After Congress Passed a Climate Change Law? Very Little." ProPublica, October 15, 2013. Retrieved July 13, 2016 (https://www.propublica.org/article /what-happened-after-congress-passed-a-climate-change-law -very-little).

Pope Francis. "Climate as a Common Good" from *Laudato Si'*. May 24, 2015. Retrieved January 8, 2016 (https://laudatosi.com/).

Queally, Jon. "Seething with Anger, Probe Demanded into Exxon's Unparalleled Climate Crime." Common Dreams, October 30, 2015. Retrieved April 27, 2016 (http://www.commondreams .org/news/2015/10/30/seething-anger-probe-demanded -exxons-unparalleled-climate-crime).

"Remarks by President Obama at the GLACIER Conference." The White House, September 1, 2015. Retrieved January 8, 2016 (https://www.whitehouse.gov/the-press-office/2015/09/01 /remarks-president-glacier-conference-anchorage-ak).

"A Reporter's Field Notes on the Coverage of Climate Change: *Yale Environment 360* Interview with Elizabeth Kolbert." *Yale Environment 360*, March 11, 2009. Retrieved January 8, 2016 (http://e360.yale.edu/feature/a_reporters_field_notes_on_the_coverage_of_climate_change/2130/).

Salamon, Margaret Klein and Ezra Silk. "The Paris Climate Talks and the 1.5C Target: Wartime-Scale Mobilization Is Our Only Option Left." Common Dreams, December 16, 2016. Retrieved January 8, 2016 (http://www.commondreams.org/views/2015/12/16/paris-climate-talks-and-15c-target-wartime-scale-mobilization-our-only-option-left).

Solomon, Lawrence. "Limited Role for CO2." *National Post*. Retrieved April 27, 2016 (http://www.nationalpost.com/story.html?id=069cb5b2-7d81-4a8e-825d-56e0f112aeb5).

Welch, Craig. "There's a Good and a Bad Way to 'Geoengineer' the Planet." *National Geographic*, February 9, 2015. Retrieved January 8, 2016 from (http://news.nationalgeographic.com/news/2015/02/150210-national-academy-geoengineering-report-climate-change-environment/).

White, Chris. "Bill Gates: The World Needs 'A Miracle' to Solve Man-Made Global Warming." The Daily Caller. February 23, 2016. Retrieved April 27, 2016 (http://dailycaller.com/2016/02/23/bill-gates-the-world-needs-a-miracle-to-solve-man-made-global-warming/).

GLOSSARY

aerosol—Tiny particles of liquid or solid materials suspended in the atmosphere. They affect how the earth absorbs energy from the sun.

anthropogenic global warming—The human-caused heating of the atmosphere by the burning of fossil fuels.

atmosphere—The whole mass of air that surrounds the Earth.

bedrock—Unbroken, solid rock under the ground.

biodiversity—The existence of many different kinds of plants and animals in an environment.

carbon emissions—The release of carbon into the atmosphere by the burning of fossil fuels.

civil disobedience—The refusal to obey certain laws, in an attempt to get the government to change them or give in to a particular demand.

climate—The average of daily weather conditions in a particular place over a long period of time.

climate denialism—The belief that climate change is not occurring.

desertification—The process land goes through as it becomes a desert, whether because of climate change or another case.

drought—A long period of dry weather.

ecosystem—All the living things, from plants and animals to microscopic organisms, that share an environment.

evaporate—To change water from a liquid to a gas (vapor).

extinction—The state at which an animal or plant species has died out completely.

fossil fuels—Fuels such as oil, gas, and coal that are formed in the earth from plant and animal remains.

frugality—Careful spending of money or resources.

geoengineering—Technologies that might be used to cool the Earth's climate.

glacier—A huge mass of ice that moves slowly down mountain valleys or over land.

greenhouse gases—Atmospheric gases including carbon dioxide, methane, nitrous oxide, and water vapor, that absorb infrared radiation from the sun, trap heat in the atmosphere, and contribute to the greenhouse effect.

Gulf Stream—The major ocean current that brings warm water north along the east coast of North America and then crosses the Atlantic to Europe, warming the air above it as it circulates.

ice sheet—A permanent layer of very thick ice ice covering a very large piece of land. These are also known as continental glaciers.

incentive—Something that encourages or motivates a spur to action.

indigenous—Existing naturally in a particular area or environment.

interglacial period—A long period of time where large ice sheets are not covering the majority of the land area. These are brought on by warming trends.

intolerance—An inability to accept or tolerate a particular item or idea.

jet stream—A narrow band of strong westerly winds moving at speeds often higher than 250 miles (400 kilometers) an hour at altitudes of 6 to 9 miles (10 to 15 kilometers).

Little Ice Age—A period of cold climate lasting from the years 1400 to about 1860 CE.

Medieval Warm Period—A warm period lasting from 1000 to about 1350 CE.

partisan—Expressing allegiance to a policial party, allowing the party to control decisions of the group.

permafrost—A permanently frozen layer of the ground at variable depth below the surface in frigid regions of the Earth.

philanthropist—An individual who works hard to help others, often through a charitable organization or organizations.

post-carbon economy—An economy not dependent for its energy needs on the burning of fossil fuels.

renewable energy—A type of energy that can be replenished without depleting resources or causing irreparable damage to the earth, such as wind power.

scientific consensus—The position generally agreed upon at a given time by most scientists specialized in a given field.

subsidy—Money provided by the government to keep a business running or to control the price of a product.

FOR MORE INFORMATION

BOOKS

Berners Lee, Mike. *The Burning Question: We Can't Burn Half the World's Oil, Coal and Gas. So How Do We Quit?* Vancouver, Greystone Books, 2013.

Colligan, L. H. *Global Warming.* Tarrytown, NY: Marshall Cavendish Benchmark Books, 2012.

Cunningham, Anne. *Climate Change: A Threat to All Life on Earth (The End of Life as We Know It).* New York: Enslow Publishing, 2016.

Espejo, Roman, Ed. *Can Glacier and Ice Melt Be Reversed?* Detroit: Greenhaven Press, 2014.

Funk, McKenzie. *Windfall: The Booming Business of Global Warming.* New York: Penguin Books, 2015.

Kallio, Jamie. *12 Things to Know About Climate Change.* North Mankato, MN: 12-Story Library, 2015.

Lawrence, Ellen. *Global Warming.* New York: Bearport Publishing, 2014.

McKibben, Bill, Ed. *The Global Warming Reader: A Century of Writing About Climate Change.* New York: Penguin Books, 2012.

McPherson, Stephanie Sammartino. *Arctic Thaw: Climate Change and the Global Race for Energy Resources.* Minneapolis: Twenty-First Century Books, 2015.

Miller, Debra A. *Global Warming.* Detroit: Greenhaven Press, 2013.

Peters, E. Kirsten. *The Whole Story of Climate: What Science Reveals About the Nature of Endless Change.* New York: Prometheus Books, 2012.

Sneideman, Joshua and Erin Twamley. *Climate Change: Discover How It Impacts Spaceship Earth.* White River Junction, VT: Nomad Press, 2015.

WEBSITES

American Solar Energy Society
www.ases.org
This nonprofit association of solar energy professionals and supporters work to inspire a new era of energy innovation, allowing an eventual transition to sustainable energy from the sun.
The ASES has existed for over 60 years, holding a yearly solar
power conference.

Centre for Renewable Energy Systems Technology (CREST)
www.lboro.ac.uk/research/crest/
CREST, based in the United Kingdom, oversees research and
development of renewable energy technology. Their research
includes study of wind power, solar power, and energy storage
in the home and business organizations. In 1994, they established a graduate program to help teach a new generation how
to build and grow sustainable energy resources.

Greenpeace USA
www.greenpeace.org/usa/en/
Founded in 1971, Greenpeace is the leading independent cam-
paigning organization that uses peaceful protest and creative
communication to expose global environmental problems and
to promote solutions that are essential to a green and peaceful
future. Greenpeace recently led the fight to stop oil drilling in
the Arctic.

Idle No More
www.idlenomore.ca
Based in Canada, Idle No More works to protect land and water
resources from large mining, logging, oil, and fishing companies, keeping them safe for Canadian First Nations people, and
ultimately all of Canada. Their National Day of Action takes
place every December 10.

Sierra Club
www.sierraclub.org
The Sierra Club was founded in 1892 by the legendary con-
servationist, naturalist, and explorer John Muir. It is now the
nation's largest and most influential grassroots environmental

organization with more than two million members and supporters. It recently led the fight to prevent the Keystone XL oil pipeline from being built.

350.org
www.350.org

Founded nearly 20 years ago by environmentalist Bill McKibben to fight climate change, 350.org is one of the main groups working for change. Activists in 189 countries have organized 350.org's local climate-focused campaigns, projects, and actions.

Union of Concerned Scientists
www.ucsusa.org

Founded more than forty years ago, the group works to refute those who claim that climate change is a hoax. The group produces reports on how the fossil fuel industry and other private interests profit from inaction on climate change.

INDEX

ABOUT THE EDITOR

Stephen Feinstein writes books on a wide variety of topics. Although he majored in art history in college, his books focus on political and scientific developments as well as cultural topics. His interests in the arts, history, and science began while he was still a child. Stephen grew up in the Bronx, and he often took advantage of New York City's wonderful museums, making frequent visits to the Museum of Natural History and its Hayden Planetarium, the Metropolitan Museum of Art, and the Museum of Modern Art. As an adult, Stephen's interest in what was going on in the world led to numerous trips abroad. The many places he visited include England, France, Netherlands, Belgium, Germany, Austria, Denmark, Italy, Greece, Switzerland, Macedonia, Serbia, Slovenia, China, and Indonesia.

For many years, Stephen worked as an editor at educational publishing companies. He eventually became a freelancer, writing educational materials for various grade levels ranging from third to twelfth grades. Stephen has lived in New York, New Jersey, San Francisco, and Seattle. Today he lives in Arizona, learning to appreciate and enjoy the desert environment.